MAKING YOUR
FAITH WORK

MAKING YOUR FAITH WORK

The principles and process of dynamic faith

Richard W. Taylor

New Wine Press

New Wine Ministries
PO Box 17
Chichester
West Sussex
United Kingdom
PO20 6YB

ISBN 1–903725–43–7

Typeset by CRB Associates, Reepham, Norfolk
Cover design by CCD, www.ccdgroup.co.uk
Printed in the United States of America

CONTENTS

DEDICATION

This book is dedicated to David and Dinah Sansome MBE. I know that without your help and support at the beginning of my journey with Christ I would not be what I am today. Your endless giving and limitless love for people continues to challenge me. Your efforts in reaching and rescuing people has its rewards in the hundreds of stories of young men and women who today have been given another chance. You will both always have a special place in my heart and my life's success is towards your reward in heaven.

ACKNOWLEDGEMENTS

No book is completed without the support of special people. I want to extend my sincere thanks to:

David Carr – my mentor who continues to push me to excel in all I do.

Yvonne East – not just my personal assistant but a fountain of wisdom. Your ability to look after my busy schedule has created the time to write, thanks!

Peter and Carole Jenkins – for your example of true faith; your guidance has steered me through many difficult times.

Tim Pettingale – your encouragement for me to write and excitement for seeing the book through to completion has been a source of real help to me.

Finally the most important people in my life, my family. Jill my wife and our beautiful children, Joshua and Caleb. Thank you for your sacrificial love in giving me the time and space to pursue God's purpose.

INTRODUCTION

Have you ever felt like faith was working for others, but not for you? For years we have been taught to conquer mountains in our lives! However, faith does not climb mountains, it *speaks* to them.

> *"For assuredly, I say to you, whoever says to this mountain, 'Be removed and be cast into the sea,' and does not doubt in his heart, but believes that those things he says will be done, he will have whatever he says."*
>
> (MARK 11:23)

Making your faith work is fundamental to living a life of victory. In this book I identify what faith is and how to put it to work. Faith does not have a formula, but it does have a *process*. Once you discover the process, you will be equipped to exercise faith in a way you have never known before.

Many think that "belief" and "faith" are the same, but they are not! I recall the story of the amazing tightrope walker, Blondin.

In 1859 the Great Blondin – the man who invented the

high wire act, announced to the world that he intended to cross Niagara Falls on a tightrope. Five thousand people, including the Prince of Wales, gathered to watch. Halfway across, Blondin suddenly stopped, steadied himself, back-flipped into the air, landed squarely on the rope, then continued safely to the other side. During that year, Blondin crossed the Falls again and again – once blindfolded, once carrying a stove, once in chains, and once on a bicycle. Just as he was about to begin yet another crossing, this time pushing a wheelbarrow, he turned to the crowd and shouted, "Who believes that I can cross pushing this wheelbarrow?" Every hand in the crowd went up. Blondin pointed at one man.

"Do you believe that I can do it?" he asked.

"Yes, I believe you can," said the man.

"Are you certain?" said Blondin.

"Yes," said the man.

"Absolutely certain?"

"Yes, absolutely certain."

"Thank you" said Blondin. "Then sir, get into the wheelbarrow."

Are you "in the wheelbarrow?" Faith is getting into the wheelbarrow. What is keeping you from getting in the wheelbarrow? I believe that as you read on, your faith will be rekindled and you will be challenged to believe God for greater things. You will move from the place of *belief* to *faith*. It's time to step out and make your faith work.

CHAPTER 1

THE POWER OF FAITH

Simply put, faith is not believing that God *can*, but that God *will*. We read in Hebrews that,

> *"Faith is the substance of things hoped for, the evidence of things not seen."*

(HEBREWS 11:1)

The root word used for "substance" is the Greek word *hypostasis* and means, "the foundation, assurance, title-deed, and guarantee of things hoped for".

So we could read the verse this way: "Now faith is the

foundation, assurance, title-deed, and guarantee of things hoped for, the evidence of things not seen."

So faith is an assurance and a guarantee! But what is that substance? Let's read on:

> *"For by it the elders obtained a good testimony. **By faith** we understand that the worlds were framed **by the word of God**, so that the things which are seen were not made of things which are visible."*
>
> (HEBREWS 11:2–3 emphasis added)

Notice that faith comes by the Word of God; therefore we must conclude that the substance of faith is God's Word. Elsewhere, Paul writes,

> *"So then faith comes by hearing, and hearing by the word of God."*
>
> (ROMANS 10:17)

FAITH IS . . .

. . . having confidence in God

In the general sense of the word, to have faith is to believe in something or someone, to fully trust, to be so confident that you base your actions on what you believe. To have faith is to be fully convinced of the truthfulness and reliability of that in which you believe.

Faith in God then, is having the kind of trust and confidence in God's Word and in Christ that leads you to commit your whole soul to Him as Savior (Justifier, Cleanser, Healer, Deliverer) and Lord (Master, King).

The NIV translation of the Hebrews scripture reads,

"Faith is being sure of what we hope for, and certain of what we do not see."

(HEBREWS 11:1 NIV)

... the substance of God's Word

Faith's substance is God's Word. When you have this substance in you, it communicates to you a certain "inner knowing" that the thing you are hoping for is certainly established, even before you see any material evidence that it has happened.

... a response that causes God to act

Faith is a spiritual force. Faith in God is a response to God's Word which moves God to act. Jesus said,

*"For assuredly I say to you, whoever **says** to this mountain, 'Be removed and cast into the sea,' and does not doubt in his heart, but **believes** that those things he **says** will be done, he will **have** whatever he **says**."*

(MARK 11:23 emphasis added)

Words mixed with real, pure faith can and will move mountains or any other problem that we face.

... from the heart

Faith in God must be from the heart. It is not merely intellectual. It is spiritual.

"For with the heart one believes unto righteousness, and with the mouth confession is made unto salvation."

(ROMANS 10:10)

... the certainty of things unseen

Faith causes you to know in your heart before you see with your eyes. Consider this poem by Ruth Morgan based on 2 Corinthians 5:7:

Sometimes I'm sad, I know not why
    My heart is sore distressed;
It seems the burdens of this world
    Have settled on my heart.

And yet I know ... I know that God
    Who doeth all things right
Will lead me thus to understand
    To walk by FAITH ... not SIGHT.

And though I may not see the way
    He's planned for me to go,
The way seems dark to me just now
    But oh, I'm sure He knows!

Today He guides my feeble step
    Tomorrow's in His right ...
He has asked me to never fear ...
    But walk by FAITH ... not SIGHT.

Some day the mists will roll away,
    The sun will shine again.
I'll see the beauty in the flowers,
    I'll hear the bird's refrain,

And then I'll know my Father's hand
   Has led the way to light
Because I placed my hand in His
   And walked by FAITH ... not SIGHT.

(Ruth A. Morgan)

Some say, "Seeing is believing." But once you see the thing you hoped for already existing in the natural order, you no longer need faith, as Paul points out:

> *"For we were saved in this hope, but hope that is seen is not hope; for why does one still hope for what he sees? But if we hope for what we do not see, we eagerly wait for it with perseverance."*
>
> (ROMANS 8:24–25)

... *birthed by hope*

Hope is a condition for faith. Hope is "a positive unwavering expectation of good". Hope is for the mind:

> *"But let us who are of the day be sober, putting on the breastplate of faith and love, and as a helmet the hope of salvation."*
>
> (1 THESSALONIANS 5:8)

The hope of salvation is described as a helmet which covers our minds. It keeps us in the place where we can believe, but it is not in itself "faith". Yet, without hope there are no "things hoped for", and therefore there cannot be faith.

... believing God has heard us

Through faith we can know we have the answer to our prayer before we see anything change in the natural order:

> *"Now this is the confidence that we have in Him, that if we ask anything according to His will, He hears us. And if we know that He hears us, whatever we ask, we know that we have the petitions that we have asked of Him."*
>
> (1 JOHN 5:14–15)

Jesus said,

> *"Therefore I say to you, whatever things you ask when you pray, believe that you receive them, and you will have them."*
>
> (MARK 11:24)

God expects us, even commands us, to believe that our petitions are answered before we make them. We must believe that the response is immediately sent **when** we pray. Faith is like the confirmation slip in our hearts that the goods are on the way. We have that confirmation slip instantly from God; we sense it in our hearts. The manifestation of those goods, the answer received, comes later as long as we are patient and do not throw away our confidence.

> *"Therefore do not cast away your confidence, which has great reward. For you have need of endurance, so that after you have done the will of God, you may receive the promise:*
>
> *'For yet a little while,
> And He who is coming will come and will not tarry.*

Now the just shall live by faith;
But if anyone draws back,
My soul has no pleasure in him.'

But we are not of those who draw back to perdition, but of those
who believe to the saving of the soul."

(HEBREWS 10:35–39)

"And we desire ... that you do not become sluggish, but imitate
those who through faith and patience inherit the promises."

(HEBREWS 6:11, 12)

... like a cheque to be cashed

Faith is like a cheque. All you have to do is hold on to the cheque, go to the bank to present it and you can confidently expect the money to appear in your account after a certain time. If you throw the cheque away the money will not be put in your account! God is trustworthy and always has the resources to back His promises.

... revealed by our actions

Living faith always has corresponding actions. We speak out what we really believe, and we act according to what we really believe. The heroes of faith like Abraham were considered men of faith because they acted on what God showed them. They acted on their faith.

"Was not Abraham our father justified by works when he
offered Isaac his son on the altar? Do you see that faith was
working together with his works, and by works faith was made
perfect? And the Scripture was fulfilled which says, 'Abraham

believed God, and it was accounted to him for righteousness.'
And he was called the friend of God."

(JAMES 2:21–23)

To live in faith means to do and say what you believe is right, without doubting.

... *rest*

Faith is a rest. It is compatible with inner peace. It is not "trying to believe". To say that you are "trying to believe" God for something is to say that you actually *don't* believe Him. The man who is "trying to believe" may be sincere, but he does not have faith.

... *an attitude*

Faith is more than a belief in God's Word, it is an attitude. Faith creates an attitude that is positive in the face of adversity.

I recall as a teenager being told things such as, "You're stupid" and "You will never do anything with your life." This bred an attitude of failure within me and it took years to reverse those thoughts. This is why Paul tells us to renew our minds to break out of the mould this world seeks to force us into:

"And do not be conformed to this world, but be transformed by
the renewing of your mind, that you may prove what is that good
and acceptable and perfect will of God."

(ROMANS 12:2)

DOUBT – THE ENEMY OF FAITH

The world's thinking will cast doubt over your ability to achieve things in God. The world's skepticism and doubt is like a cancer on the human soul. But how do we remove doubt from our life?

The most important thing you can do is to renew your mind by continually feeding it with the Word of God. Thinking that you will never be able to accomplish anything will keep you from God's purpose. Having doubt in your life is a major downfall. You can't accomplish anything without having the "God kind" of faith. If you are praying and believing for a new job or gaining financial stability it requires you to have faith. Thoughts of doubt will develop into negative actions.

THE CURSE OF NEGATIVE THINKING

We usually have negativity in our life from a lack of confidence – and our lack of confidence stems from the fact that we often don't believe what God's Word says about us. The first thing you have to do to build your confidence is to believe that you are a child of God. When you dwell on this truth you will begin to see that, with God's help, you can accomplish anything in your life.

"I can do all things through Christ who strengthens me."
(PHILIPPIANS 4:13)

Scripture tells us that when we are born again, we are no longer victims but victors.

"Yet in all these things we are more than conquerors through Him who loved us."

(ROMANS 8:37)

Develop the attitude of faith that says, "I can do all things." Once you decide this, nothing can stop you. By keeping your mind trained to have faith you are removing all the negativity from your life. Surround yourself with faith-filled positive people. If you spend a lot of time around negative people, then you will become negative too.

It takes time to develop a faith-filled mind. Once you decide that you don't want negativity in your life any more and disconnect yourself from the people who have nothing but negative thoughts and words, you can begin to grow as a person of faith. Whenever something happens in your life, don't automatically think negatively about the situation, no matter what it is. Practice faith and eventually this will become a part of you.

Some people are born with a constantly positive outlook on life, but most of us need to work on it. Maintaining a positive attitude will help you to find the faith with which you can fulfill your destiny. You will not find any successful leader who has not mastered this concept.

Here are a few ideas to help you remain faith-filled and positive in your every day life:

- Associate with winners. Your peers should be people who are and want to be successful. They should be the type of people who through faith have achieved things that God inspired them to do.

- Wipe away those things that blur your faith. Has your view of the future been blurred by negative thoughts?
- Clean out all your emotional clutter on a regular basis. If someone wronged you in the past, forgive him or her. Unforgiveness will hinder your faith.
- Focus on faith as a solution instead of the problem.
- Avoid telling yourself negative things. There will be enough negativity assaulting you from external sources. Why let it come from within too?
- We all have negative thoughts from time to time. The best way I have found to counteract your negative thoughts is by quoting the Word of God.
- Think back upon a time you have successfully dealt with a similar problem and how God brought you through. This will give you faith and confidence in God to handle the current situation.

Above all else, you have to have a lot of confidence in God. Not arrogance, but confidence, knowing that you have the skills, talent and intelligence given to you by God to be victorious in whatever life has in store for you.

Whatever challenges you face, *focus on the future* rather than on the past. Faith always looks forward. Get a clear mental image of your ideal successful future, and then take steps of faith in that direction. Get your mind, your thoughts, and your mental images focused on the future by faith.

Whenever you're faced with a difficulty, *focus on the solution* rather than on the problem. Think and confess the Word as your solution, rather than wasting time rehashing and reflecting on the problem. Solutions are inherently positive, whereas problems are inherently negative. The instant that you begin thinking and confessing the Word of faith in terms of solutions, circumstance has to give way to change!

Believe that something good is hidden within each difficulty or challenge. Dr. Norman Vincent Peale, a major proponent of positive thinking, once said, "Whenever God wants to give us a gift, he wraps it up in a problem." The bigger the gift you have coming, the bigger the problem you will receive! But the wonderful thing is that if you look for the gift, you will always find it.

Remember that whatever situation you are facing at the moment, it is exactly the right situation you need to develop faith. This situation has been sent to you to help you learn something about faith, to help you expand and grow.

You can be a person of faith if you simply think about the future, confess the Word and look for the good. If you do what other great men and women of faith have done, use your faith to exert control over the situation, you will be amazed what God can do. And you will reap the benefits of the power of faith.

CHAPTER 2

THE PROCESS OF FAITH

"It is the heart that senses God, and not the reason.
That is what faith is: God perceptible
to the heart and not to reason."
(Blaise Pascal)

This is the largest chapter in the book because if you fail to understand this process then you will fail to know how faith works.

"So then faith comes by hearing, and hearing by the word of God."
(ROMANS 10:17)

It is God's Word that creates faith to perform the impossible, making it possible. However, we must understand that faith has a process. To suggest faith has no process and is something intangible and mysterious is ridiculous, because each time an act of faith is recorded in the Bible, there is visibly a process at work. I describe this process as consisting of four clear steps:

- **Hear it**
- **See it**
- **Say it**
- **Seize it**

The book of Numbers records the account of God promising a land of blessing and prosperity for His people under the leadership of Moses. Here we can identify the process of faith at work.

> *"And the LORD **spoke** to Moses, saying, 'Send men to **spy** out the land of Canaan, which I am giving to the children of Israel; from each tribe of their fathers you shall send a man, every one a leader among them."*
>
> (NUMBERS 13:1–2 emphasis added)

STEP 1: HEARING

Hearing is the first step in the process of faith – to hear from God. We read that, *"the LORD spoke to Moses"* and Moses *heard* the Lord. Many people today are attempting great things in ministry, but have not actually received a mandate from God for what they are doing. You cannot build on a good idea or a nice thought anything that will stand the test unless you have *heard from God.*

Christians get frustrated and discouraged as they try to establish a work for God out of their own desire and not from the commissioning voice of God. The question should not be what can we do for God, but what has God said to us? Not the church down the road, but us!

STEP 2: SEEING

Once we have heard God's voice we are left with no doubt and faith begins to grow. The second stage in the process is to then *see*. We read that Moses sent the men out to *spy* and to *see* the land: *"Send men to spy out the land of Canaan ... "*

Faith is more than hearing, it is seeing with the eye of your inward man. What are you "seeing" right now? It's time to begin seeing your victory, seeing your blessing, seeing your destiny and to start living in it today.

In this process of faith you can only receive what you can see. We refuse to see the mountain of lack, the mountain of depression, the mountain of failure, but with the eyes of faith we see the fruit of the land, blessing, healing, deliverance, prosperity and the ability to overcome and accomplish God's purpose for our lives.

Out of the twelve spies sent to *see*, ten came back with a negative report on the land. They only saw the giants that occupied the land, yet two men, Joshua and Caleb, saw the opportunity for incredible blessing and an exciting future in a land that had been given to them by God.

It's amazing that even in our churches today we have

Canaan Christians who tend to see the potential and blessing in a situation, and Egypt Christians who don't tend to see what you can see! Egypt Christians tend to only see and live in what they know and are comfortable with. They are not prepared to chart new territory and face the adventure of pioneering the awesome things that God has promised – they are content with staying where they are until they die. But God is calling people to live at higher levels of faith and victory.

As soon as we have heard from God, we must have a vision for what He is calling us to do. We must see His promise just as Joshua and Caleb saw the land.

STEP 3: SAYING

Thirdly, for faith to be operative there has to be a confession. You have what you say. Notice Caleb's attitude:

> *"Then Caleb quieted the people before Moses, and said, 'Let us go up at once and take possession, for we are well able to overcome it.' "*
>
> (NUMBERS 13:30)

Caleb had heard the promise, he had seen the land, and now he was ready to speak out! He made a confession based on what he had heard and seen, and his confession was one of action: *"Let us go up at once and take possession ... "*

"Let's go and seize it now," was Caleb's declaration. Hear it, See it, Say it, Seize it! Are you getting the picture?

Faith must have an element of confession attached to it. The Bible has a lot to say about the creative power of words. For instance, in Proverbs we read about the potential for words to create blessing or cursing:

"Death and life are in the power of the tongue,
And those who love it will eat its fruit."

(PROVERBS 18:21)

I've always been amazed by this verse of Scripture:

"For assuredly, I say to you, whoever says to this mountain, 'Be removed and be cast into the sea,' and does not doubt in his heart, but believes that those things he says will be done, he will have whatever he says."

(MARK 11:23)

Here we see that the words we speak in faith have power: *"He will have whatever he **says**."* But this does not give us license to confess and ask for things that God has not promised. Remember the process: you first have to hear from God, then you have to see with the eyes of faith, and then confess with your mouth what you have heard and see, calling it into existence. Faith is the confession of our substance.

If God has promised it, then we can confess it with confidence. For example, healing belongs to us because God has declared it in His Word. We can speak health over our lives because the Bible informs us,

"He was wounded for our transgressions,
He was bruised for our iniquities;
The chastisement for our peace was upon Him,
And by His stripes we are healed."

(ISAIAH 53:5)

STEP 4: SEIZING

Finally we have to seize the promise. Remember what God told Joshua?

> *"Moses My servant is dead. Now therefore, **arise, go** over this Jordan, you and all this people, to the land which I am giving to them — the children of Israel. Every place that the sole of your foot will tread upon I have given you, as I said to Moses."*
>
> (JOSHUA 1:2–3 emphasis added)

Moses heard the call, Joshua and Caleb saw the land, Caleb said, "Let us go", and eventually they took the land!

THE TESTING OF WHAT WE HAVE HEARD

We must expect however, that this process in our lives, especially when it comes to acts of great faith, will be attacked. James wrote,

> *"My brethren, count it all joy when you fall into various trials, knowing that the **testing of your faith** produces patience. But let patience have its perfect work, that you may be perfect and complete, lacking nothing."*
>
> (JAMES 1:2–4 emphasis added)

When God has spoken to you and you are believing Him for something, guard yourself from negative conversations that will rob you of your faith, instead of inspiring it. The devil does not want you to hear the *word*! God's word to you is the seed that produces faith. The devil's plan therefore, is to kill the seed. In Genesis chapter 3, Satan attacked what Eve had heard and distorted the words God had spoken to her:

> *"Now the serpent was more cunning than any beast of the field which the LORD God had made. And he said to the woman,* **'Has God indeed said***, "You shall not eat of every tree of the garden"?"*

(GENESIS 3:1 emphasis added)

Now, listen to Jesus' perspective in the parable of the sower:

> *"And when a great multitude had gathered, and they had come to Him from every city, He spoke by a parable: 'A sower went out to sow his* **seed***. And as he sowed, some fell by the wayside; and it was trampled down, and the birds of the air devoured it. Some fell on rock; and as soon as it sprang up, it withered away because it lacked moisture. And some fell among thorns, and the thorns sprang up with it and choked it. But others fell on good ground, sprang up, and yielded a crop a hundredfold.' When He had said these things He cried, 'He who has ears to hear, let him hear!'*
>
> *Then His disciples asked Him, saying, 'What does this parable mean?' And He said, 'To you it has been given to know the mysteries of the kingdom of God, but to the rest it is given in parables, that*
>
> > *"Seeing they may not see,*
> > *And hearing they may not understand."*

Now the parable is this: **The seed is the word of God.**
*Those by the wayside are the ones who hear; then the devil comes
and takes away the word out of their hearts, lest they should
believe and be saved. But the ones on the rock are those who,
when they hear, receive the word with joy; and these have no
root, who believe for a while and in time of temptation fall away.
Now the ones that fell among thorns are those who, when they
have heard, go out and are choked with cares, riches, and
pleasures of life, and bring no fruit to maturity. But the ones
that fell on the good ground are those who, having heard the
word with a noble and good heart, keep it and bear fruit with
patience.' "*

(LUKE 8:4–15 emphasis added)

The seed is the word of God. Notice that Jesus is dealing
with the destruction of the seed. Your faith is attacked when
the enemy seeks to take away the word that you have heard
from God.

The second group in the parable of the sower are those
who believe for a while, but when the going gets tough they
have no root. In terms of the process of faith, this would be
someone who has only had an emotional, "I believe" kind
of experience and whose faith wavers.

*"... and these have no root, who believe for a while and in time
of temptation fall away."*

(LUKE 8:13)

The third group in the parable are those who listen but
never come to maturity. These may be those who are inter-
ested in Jesus' message, but who cannot accept it because of

their devotion to material things, life's worries, riches, and pleasures.

> *"Now the ones that fell among thorns are those who, when they have heard, go out and are choked with cares, riches, and pleasures of life, and bring no fruit to maturity."*
>
> (LUKE 8:14)

Notice that Jesus pinpoints the issues of "cares, riches, and the pleasures of life" as stumbling blocks to a life of faith. Sometimes a walk of faith requires you to give things away and have a liberal spirit. It means we should not be so attached to material things that they are a hindrance to our faith.

But there is one more fundamental issue that is a major stumbling block to faith. It is a tool in the devil's hand that he has used against believers for centuries and it is still as effective today as it has ever been: *worry*!

Jesus told His disciples,

> *"Therefore I say to you, do not worry about your life, what you will eat; nor about the body, what you will put on. Life is more than food, and the body is more than clothing. Consider the ravens, for they neither sow nor reap, which have neither storehouse nor barn; and God feeds them. Of how much more value are you than the birds? And which of you by worrying can add one cubit to his stature? If you then are not able to do the least, why are you anxious for the rest? Consider the lilies, how they grow: they neither toil nor spin; and yet I say to you, even Solomon in all his glory was not arrayed like one of these. If then God so clothes the grass, which today is in the field and tomorrow*

is thrown into the oven, how much more will He clothe you, O you of little faith?"

(LUKE 12:22–28)

Jesus spent a lot of time telling His disciples not to worry. He even connects a lack of faith to worry. By worrying you highlight your lack of faith and trust in God's Word.

The fourth group of people in Jesus' parable are those who hear the word and reap a harvest:

" 'But others fell on good ground, sprang up, and yielded a crop a hundredfold.' When He had said these things He cried, 'He who has ears to hear, let him hear!' "

(LUKE 8:8)

The condition of our hearts is measured by the faith that's in our soil! The Word when mixed with faith creates dynamic results.

THE TESTING OF WHAT WE SEE

We are to walk by faith and not by sight. That means we don't see impossibilities, but opportunities for faith to work. For our faith to grow it is vital that we see God for who He really is. Once we understand how big God is and how much He wants to do for us, His children, then our faith will flourish. But it is also important that we see ourselves as God sees us. If we had a true revelation of all that God has made us and given us in Christ, then that would transform our faith! The apostle Paul tells us,

"If anyone is in Christ, he is a new creation; old things have passed away; behold, all things have become new ... we are ambassadors for Christ, as though God were pleading through us: we implore you on Christ's behalf, be reconciled to God. For He made Him who knew no sin to be sin for us, that we might become the righteousness of God in Him."

(2 CORINTHIANS 5:17, 20–21)

We are not the same as we used to be because in Christ we are new creations. We think, act and speak differently. Our struggles are no longer impossible to overcome. We are made *new*!

You are no longer a person of insignificance. God says that you are His ambassador on earth. Your life matters! In the face of adversity stand up as an ambassador of Christ.

In Christ you are now seen as righteous before God. Righteousness is more than "doing what is right", it is "being what is right". We were never designed to be human "doings", but human "beings". What we are in Christ affects the way we live. You are the righteousness of God not because of what you do, but because of what you have received through Calvary.

*"... be found in Him, not having my own righteousness, which is from the law, but that which is through faith in Christ, the righteousness which is from God **by faith**."*

(PHILIPPIANS 3:9 emphasis added)

How we see ourselves will determine the level of victory we see in our lives. The Bible calls us to live our lives "by faith". You may not see yourself living a life a victory, but it is your right as a believer amongst trial, tragedy, and a world filled with ungodliness, to live a life of spiritual victory. As Jesus Himself declared,

> *"The thief does not come except to steal, and to kill, and to destroy.* **I have come that they may have life, and that they may have it more abundantly."**
>
> (JOHN 10:10 emphasis added)

As what we have "seen" in the spirit is tested, here are some things to remember about faith:

▶ *Faith does not dismiss circumstances, but looks for the path of opportunity*

When everything seems impossible and outside of your ability to change it, then it is no longer down to you to solve! It is an opportunity for God to move. Faith never gives in, but presses through to solutions. Faith stands with a mountain in front of it and sees beyond the mountain into the Promised Land.

▶ *Faith sees hardship as process*

Many people reading this will be in the midst of the process of faith – believing for something you have "seen" but which has not yet come to fruition. During the time between the promise and the fulfillment we might have to endure hardship as we battle towards the goal. Not all these battles are from the devil, some are "allowed" by heaven. They are allowed because God's ultimate goal is to develop character in you to bring you evermore towards Christlikeness.

Sometimes God directs the circumstances of your life in order to get you from point A to point B.

► *Faith makes sure your failures are never final*
Failure in the life of faith is never final, because faith refuses to give up. In fact, failure is faith's opportunity. For example, when Paul and Silas had been arrested for preaching Jesus, they found themselves in prison awaiting trial. What seemed to be an end to their ministry was only the start. Faith saw an opportunity to reveal God's omnipotent power.

► *Faith is the conqueror over fear*
When fear attempts to paralyze you, take the shield of faith, confess the Word of God, and bring the giant down.

Not only is what we see about ourselves and our future tested, but there also comes the testing of our declaration of faith.

THE TESTING OF WHAT WE SAY

We are often discouraged from speaking faith over our circumstances, but as believers we should speak things up. The Bible has much to say about the power of confession and speaking out. Speak the Word over your challenges.

> *"For with the heart one believes unto righteousness, and with the mouth confession is made unto salvation."*
>
> (ROMANS 10:10)

Confessing Christ as your living Lord and Savior with your mouth releases God's salvation into your life. And since salvation includes many benefits and blessings, making sure that we continue to confess our faith with our mouths is a major key to receiving what God has provided for us by His grace.

As it says in Proverbs,

"Death and life are in the power of the tongue,
And those who love it will eat its fruit."

(PROVERBS 18:21)

The power of the tongue is in the power of the words we speak. All our words have an effect on the spiritual atmosphere around us, either for good or bad. It is through words that covenants and promises are established. It is through words that our faith or our fears are expressed. Bad words open the door for bad spirits to be at work. Good words open the door for God and His angels to be at work.

Words are spiritual seeds. Words of life produce life; words of faith produce faith; words of love produce love; words of hope produce hope, and so on. Words of death attract spirits of death; words of doubt attract doubt; words of fear attract spirits of fear, and so on. We must guard carefully what we *say*. The Bible has a lot to say on this subject, especially in the Book of Proverbs. Meditate on the following scriptures:

"In the multitude of words sin is not lacking,
But he who restrains his lips is wise.
The tongue of the righteous is choice silver;
The heart of the wicked is worth little.

The lips of the righteous feed many,
But fools die for lack of wisdom."

(PROVERBS 10:19–21)

"There is one who speaks like the piercings of a sword,
But the tongue of the wise promotes health.
The truthful lip shall be established forever,
But a lying tongue is but for a moment."

(PROVERBS 12:18–19)

"A soft answer turns away wrath,
But a harsh word stirs up anger.
The tongue of the wise uses knowledge rightly,
But the mouth of fools pours forth foolishness.
The eyes of the LORD are in every place,
Keeping watch on the evil and the good.
A wholesome tongue is a tree of life,
But perverseness in it breaks the spirit."

(PROVERBS 15:1–4)

Jesus said,

"But I say to you that for every idle word men may speak, they
will give account of it on the day of judgment. For by your words
you will be justified, and by your words you will be condemned."
(MATTHEW 12:36–37)

And Paul said,

*"And **whatever** you do, **in word** or deed, do **all** in the name of*
the Lord Jesus, giving thanks to God the Father through Him."
(COLOSSIANS 3:17 emphasis added)

Confession in Greek is the word *homologeo* and it means literally "to say the same thing". To confess the Word of God then means to say the same thing as God's Word says. When you say it, it tends to produce faith because in saying it you must also hear it from your own mouth, and hearing the Word causes faith to come (Romans 10:17). In speaking out the Word, you identify and align *yourself* with the truth of God's Word. The more you speak God's Word, the more you will believe it, and the more you believe it, the more faith will work for you.

> *"A man's stomach shall be satisfied from the fruit of his*
> *   mouth,*
> *From the produce of his lips he shall be filled."*
>
> (PROVERBS 18:20)

This means that we feed on the words we speak. What we say comes back to affect our own heart and our own spiritual condition. That is another reason why confessing the Word and not negative things will greatly help our faith.

At times it is difficult to speak consistently with what the Bible says, because our minds are not sufficiently renewed. We still have doubt in our souls. We must reprogram our subconscious minds to accept God's principles and God's promises without doubt.

> *"Do not be conformed to this world, but be transformed by the*
> *renewing of your mind, that you may prove what is that good and*
> *acceptable and perfect will of God."*
>
> (ROMANS 12:2)

Meditation, repeated pondering, listening to good preaching, confessing the Word, as well as informed study will help. The Word must enter deeply into us. This will change the way we are, the way we speak, the way we respond to difficulties and challenges. If it does not, we have been too superficial in our treatment of the Word. We have substituted only a "head" knowledge and recognition of the Word for real meditation and confession leading to a "heart" knowledge.

God talks in faith:

"God ... gives life to the dead and calls those things which do not exist as though they did."

(ROMANS 4:17)

Through faith-filled words, God created the universe:

"By faith we understand that the worlds were framed by the word of God, so that the things which are seen were not made of things which are visible."

(HEBREWS 11:3)

God's words produce actions and as children of God we are called to be imitators of God (Ephesians 5:1–18). When we are in Christ and we have the promise of God, we have the right to speak about something God has promised as if it existed, even before our natural senses are conscious of it. It is our faith that gives substance to this confession of things not seen. For example, if we have believed God for a car, we can talk about our car before we see it. We should realize that God has already, *"given us all things that pertain to life and godliness"* (2 Peter 1:3) and all spiritual blessings (Ephesians 1:3). But the effective receiving depends on our faith. Faith is confident of the faithfulness of God in His declared promises and talks and acts so, even before the natural eye sees.

Your tongue has the power to create

Just as God spoke the world into being, so He expects us to use the creative power in our words by speaking out our faith. God created mankind with creative ability, in His likeness. James understands the creative power of the tongue, when he describes how it can shape your life:

> *"Indeed, we put bits in horses' mouths that they may obey us, and we turn their whole body. Look also at ships: although they are so large and are driven by fierce winds, they are turned by a very small rudder wherever the pilot desires."*
>
> (JAMES 3:3–4)

We have to make a decision every single day to confess blessing and victory over our families, over each other, our leaders and our churches.

Confession of faith is not an acceptance of the present, but a vision of the future

Men and women who live by faith acknowledge their present, but refuse to accept it as their future. Read these amazing words from Hebrews 11:

> *"These all died in faith, not having received the promises, but having seen them afar off were assured of them, embraced them*

*and confessed that they were strangers and pilgrims on the earth.
For those who say such things declare plainly that they seek a
homeland. And truly if they had called to mind that country
from which they had come out, they would have had opportunity
to return. But now they desire a better, that is, a heavenly
country. Therefore God is not ashamed to be called their God, for
He has prepared a city for them."*

(Hebrews 11:13–16)

In your life right now you may need healing, you may
need a financial miracle, or a change in your circumstances.
Some aspects of these things may be subject to decisions
that you need to make, but when things are out of your
control, faith has to step in with bold confession and say,
"I'm not staying like this any more because God has more
in store for my life."

Mark's gospel tells the story of a woman with a blood
issue who approached and touched Jesus who displayed this
kind of attitude. She simply did not accept her present
circumstances as final, she had faith to be healed.

*"Now a certain woman had a flow of blood for twelve years, and
had suffered many things from many physicians. She had spent all
that she had and was no better, but rather grew worse. When she
heard about Jesus, she came behind Him in the crowd and
touched His garment. For she said, 'If only I may touch His
clothes, I shall be made well.' Immediately the fountain of her
blood was dried up, and she felt in her body that she was healed of
the affliction ... [Jesus] said to her, 'Daughter, your faith has
made you well. Go in peace, and be healed of your affliction.'"*

(Mark 5:25–29, 34)

This woman had spent all she had on medical help, but nothing had worked. Eventually she heard that Jesus was in town and probably had been told of the miracles He performed, so she set out to find Him and ask for healing.

What was the greatest contributing factor to her eventual healing? *Faith.*

> *"And He said to her, 'Daughter, your faith has made you well. Go in peace, and be healed of your affliction.'"*
>
> (Mark 5:34)

Jesus told the woman that it was *her faith* that had made her well, and connected her faith to the miracle.

It's no surprise that faith is connected to miracles. A miracle in and of itself is an act of pure faith. To believe for that which is impossible is the very essence of faith! The woman with the issue of blood had faith that she could be healed and refused to accept her current circumstances as the final word. Her faith was rewarded!

LEARN TO CONFESS THE WORD OVER YOUR PROBLEMS

God's Word in you is greater than the problem in front of you. But if you don't' know the Word then how can you confess it? You must know what God's Word says, because this is the basis for your authority as a child of God.

Your problem may say, *"You can't"*, but the Word says, *"I can do all things through Christ."*

Your problem may say, *"You're powerless"*, but the Word says, *"Greater is He that is in me than he that is in the world."*

Your problem may say, *"You are staying sick"*, but the Word says, *"By His stripes I am healed."*

Your problem may say, *"You cannot pay your bills"*, but the Word says, *"My God shall supply all my needs according to His riches in glory."*

DON'T GIVE LIFE TO LIMITING CONFESSION OVER YOU

If people have spoken and confessed limitations over you, do not give life to their words. Refuse to let them occupy your mind. Fill your mind with God's Word and His plan for your future.

Notice God said to Abraham,

"I will bless those who bless you,
And I will curse him who curses you."

(GENESIS 12:3)

This applies to every born again person. When people intend to limit your life by words of hatred, jealousy and spite it will come back upon their own lives. Be careful therefore, not to confess things about other people that could rebound on you!

GOD'S CONFESSION OVER YOUR LIFE IS TO BRING YOU INTO BLESSING

"For I know the thoughts that I think toward you, says the LORD, thoughts of peace and not of evil, to give you a future and a hope."

(JEREMIAH 29:11)

Above all, remember that God wants to bless you! If you can grasp this and allow it to work in your life you will experience victory and become a true man or woman of faith.

CHAPTER 3

THE CHARACTER OF FAITH

Our faith tends to be idle when all the circumstances of our life are peaceful and harmonious. Only when circumstances are adverse is one's faith in God really exercised.

Faith, like muscle, grows strong and supple with exercise. When faith is operating in your life you develop what I call "faith's character". Faith refuses to give up in the face of adversity and is not frightened by obstacles. It displays a strong determination to keep believing, despite the circumstances.

I'm reminded of the story of a farmer who bought a piece of land to grow and harvest crops. Having bought the land as an investment he was soon left feeling as if it was a bad investment. At the top of the field lay a huge rock that was stopping the flow of water which would give nourishment to the field and help produce a healthy crop. The year of harvest came and due to a lack of irrigation the farmer failed to produce any harvest.

Such was his disappointment that he decided to take a sledge hammer, stand on the rock and begin pounding away to try to remove it. To his amazement, only little pieces splintered off the rock and it stayed intact. He rained down hundreds of blows on it, but it seemingly had no effect. After exhausting himself he decided to give up.

That evening he thought he heard a voice say to him to go back and try hitting the rock again. So he took his sledge hammer, climbed the obstacle and as he threw the hammer down the rock split into two on his first blow. The obstacle was overcome and he later harvested a great crop.

The story displays the character of faith. Many of us give up far too early. We make excuses like, "I tried it before and it didn't work!" Try again! The farmer did and his determination helped him to overcome the obstacle that was preventing him from bringing in a great harvest.

Remember the woman in the previous chapter with the blood issue? She had waited twelve years to be healed. She never gave up believing and God rewarded her faith when Jesus came to her town. Her determination showed her degree of faith. Your determination will also determine your degree of faith. The Bible says that we have been given *"a measure"* of faith (Romans 12:3) and as we exercise that faith, it grows.

Another characteristic of faith is *confidence*. Faith is confident of a good outcome. The Bible says,

> *"Being confident of this very thing, that He who has begun a good work in you will complete it until the day of Jesus Christ"*
>
> (PHILIPPIANS 1:6)

Our lives are not to be measured by what we've done, or where we are now, but where we are going. Faith looks forward and is confident that God will work all things together for good. Faith gives birth to a "God-kind" of confidence that many misinterpret. Sometimes, when I have stood confidently believing God with bold confessions of faith, others have accused me of being arrogant. But I know that if my God said it, I believe it, and that settles the matter.

Paul preached the kingdom of God with confidence,

> *"Then Paul dwelt two whole years in his own rented house, and received all who came to him, preaching the kingdom of God and teaching the things which concern the Lord Jesus Christ with all **confidence**, no one forbidding him."*
>
> (ACTS 28:30–31 emphasis added)

Faith has a confidence that refuses to bow to adversity, because if we confidently hold fast to God's Word and our confession we shall overcome.

> *"Therefore do not cast away your confidence, which has great reward."*
>
> (HEBREWS 10:35)

Another characteristic of faith is *trust*.

Every Saturday we go as a family to a country club that has leisure facilities. My sons Joshua and Caleb both love swimming. They are still very young and have to wear inflated arm bands. On one particular Saturday I wanted to teach Joshua, our eldest, to swim without the aid of his arm bands. As I sat him on the edge of the pool and took them off I said to him, "Trust me son. Dad wouldn't want to hurt you would he?" "No" he replied sheepishly. I held his chest as he kicked his little legs and swung his arms. Without him knowing I slowly took away my hand from his chest and he actually was doing it by himself. However, after a yard or so he realized what I had done and began to panic, shouting "Daddy, Daddy"! I put my hand back on his chest, much to his relief, and told him, "It's OK, Daddy's here!"

Faith is no different. It's time we all took off our spiritual arm bands, got out of our comfort zones, and learned to trust our heavenly Father, believing that His hand will always be there for provision and safety. Faith trusts God implicitly through times of change and chaos. Faith *always* trusts.

CHAPTER 4

THE ENEMIES OF FAITH

Faith is to accept the impossible, do without the indispensable, and bear the intolerable. When you start to move in the God-kind of faith, watch out for the enemy! Faith has enemies that are assigned to assassinate your walk with God. One of the first and most formidable enemies I want to deal with in this chapter is *doubt*.

*"Jesus answered and said to them, 'Have faith in God. For assuredly, I say to you, whoever says to this mountain, "Be removed and be cast into the sea," and does not **doubt** in his heart, but believes that those things he says will be done, he will*

have whatever he says. Therefore I say to you, whatever things you ask when you pray, believe that you receive them, and you will have them.' "

(MARK 11:22–24 emphasis added)

These are the words of Jesus. Notice again in this verse that faith has a confession – "... *whoever* **says** *to this mountain ...* " While Jesus is teaching His disciples about the power of confession, He says in verse 23, "... *and does not doubt in his heart ...* " Faith is often hindered by doubt.

ENEMY NUMBER 1: DOUBT

Faith and Doubt

Doubt sees the obstacles.
  Faith sees the way!
Doubt sees the darkest night,
  Faith sees the day!
Doubt dreads to take a step.
  Faith soars on high!
Doubt questions, "Who believes?"
  Faith answers, "I!"

(Anonymous)

The first enemy of faith is *doubt*. Doubt can come in a number of guises, one of which is adverse circumstances. If you are facing what seem to be impossible circumstances in your family, finances, ministry, career, or with your health, these circumstances can speak doubt into your dreams and purposes.

Doubt pours water over the passionate fire that keeps your dreams alive. I remember one pastor friend saying to me, "Richard, keep the fire burning!" and I have sought to do that. But, there have been times when circumstances have pressured me to give in and stop believing. At those times you need to let your faith rise up within you and declare, *"Greater is He that is in me than he who is in the world"* (see 1 John 4:4).

Doubt is based on circumstantial evidence

Doubt is never fact, but fantasy. It only exists because we allow it to. We can decide to destroy doubt immediately that it enters our minds. If you are believing God for a new house, a child, or a job, faith says, *"My God shall supply all my needs according to His riches in glory"* (see Philippians 4:19). Doubt comes along with circumstantial evidence and says to you, "You don't have any money for a house, you don't have the qualifications for that job, and you can't have children because of what the doctor says!" We are not meant to live under such accusations of doubt. Instead we are to take God at His word.

Doubt is satanically inspired

In chapter 2 we looked briefly at the Genesis account of the Fall, where Satan sought to distort the words that God had spoken to Adam and Eve. Another of his key tactics is to sow seeds of doubt in our minds to undermine what God has said to us. In Genesis chapter 3 we see him doing just that as he tries to persuade Eve that she has not heard God correctly.

God had instructed Adam and Eve not to eat of the tree of knowledge or they would die.

> *"And out of the ground the LORD God made every tree grow that is pleasant to the sight and good for food. The tree of life was also in the midst of the garden, and the tree of the knowledge of good and evil."*
> (GENESIS 2:9)

> *"But of the tree of the knowledge of good and evil you shall not eat, for in the day that you eat of it you shall surely die."*
> (GENESIS 2:17)

Satan came along and placed doubt in their minds by casting doubt upon God's word:

> *"Now the serpent was more cunning than any beast of the field which the LORD God had made. And he said to the woman, 'Has God indeed said, "You shall not eat of every tree of the garden"?'"*
> (GENESIS 3:1)

"Has God really said ...?" "Are you *sure* He said that?" are familiar phrases in the devil's vocabulary. Satan successfully inspired doubt in Eve's mind and it was enough to derail her faith in God's word.

What about Peter in the New Testament? He tried to cast doubt upon the need for Jesus to go to the cross. Jesus responded to him by saying, *"Get thee behind me, Satan!"* (see Matthew 16:23 KJV). You have to tell your doubt to get behind you because it does not belong in your future.

Doubt stops miracles in your life
Jesus had returned to His home town after traveling,

preaching and performing miracles all around the country.
But the scripture says of His home town,

*"Now He did not do many mighty works there because of their
unbelief."*

(MATTHEW 13:58)

Unbelief and doubt can stop miracles from happening.
Those who knew Jesus during His formative years saw Him
as "the carpenter's son". They judged Him based on the
person they *used to know*. There are times in my own life
when I have seen old colleagues judge me based on the
person I used to be. They do not realize that I have moved
on into newer and better things.

Doubt is an enemy to faith because it speaks with a voice
that challenges the truth or the reliability of what we should
be believing. To overcome doubt we must fill ourselves
with the Word of God, meditating on it deeply and
repetitively. Doubt is the evidence of an unconsecrated
heart and mind. It is the evidence of a lack of devotion to
God's Word. Doubt, like fear, torments. We must forgive
others and give our whole hearts to God. We must stop
listening to the voice of our own carnal mind which has
been trained from early days to resist God. This is a
decision. Doubt will never be fully overcome until we treat
the Bible as God's final word on the matter.

ENEMY NUMBER 2: UNFORGIVENESS

Another enemy of faith is *unforgiveness*. Once I was speaking
with a single mother about forgiveness. She had been

divorced and was having to work to support herself and three young children. She told me that since her husband had walked out on them, every month she struggled to pay the bills. She was very bitter about the separation and divorce, but I was urging her to forgive her husband. She said to me, "I have to tell my kids all the time that we have no money to go to the cinema or to go on holidays. How can you tell me to forgive him?"

I answered her, "I'm not asking you to forgive him because what he did was acceptable. It wasn't. It was mean and selfish. I'm asking you to forgive him because he doesn't deserve the power to live in your head and turn you into a bitter, angry woman. You're not hurting *him* by holding on to that resentment, but you are hurting *yourself*."

If we are holding on to issues of past hurts and things that others have done to us, then faith cannot work. You must not allow your mind to be consumed with things that were done to you! Fill your mind with the fact you are bigger than the hurt and your future is far more important.

I have advised so many people that have been trapped by unforgiveness from their past. They live in prisons of containment; their minds are caged and have no freedom to fly! Make a decision today to forgive and move on and live in faith.

Here are some good reasons why you should forgive others:

- It sets you free from your past
- It gives you the power to face future hurt
- It stops you developing a bitter and critical attitude
- It allows faith to work for you

The worse kind of attitude to have in life is one of bitterness. Bitterness is the cancer that eats away at faith-filled life. Deal with it now, or it will deal with you! Forgive and forge ahead into your God-given dreams and potential.

ENEMY NUMBER 3: FEAR

The next enemy of faith is *fear*. Growing up as I did in an environment of poverty and violence, fear was always knocking at my door. Thank God that after some years and a radical conversion to Christ, my fears lost their grip on me.

Throughout history the mark of true heroism has not been characterized by men and women who were not afraid. Rather, heroism has been epitomized by men and women who faced their fears, acted in spite of them, and overcame in faith, breaking the stranglehold of fear on their lives.

You need to realize that fear is going to exist and maintain its control on your life, *until* you face it. Once you face it *you* will gain control and your fear will falter, lessening its grip on your life.

Make facing your fear a part of your daily life and remember that faith does not back down. Consciously and continuously take steps to chip away at that fear by exercising your faith. Look at every situation or task that induces fear in you as a challenge, or an opportunity, for you to prove God's Word. If you *do* those things that you fear over and over again, your fear will lose its hold on you.

Zig Ziglar put it well when he gave the following definition of fear:

"Fear = F.E.A.R or 'False Evidence Appears Real.'"

There have been moments in my own life where I have had to make courageous decisions for my future. Each time pessimism would lurk and whisper things like, "It won't work" and "Who do you think you are?" My response was always the same: *"I can do all things through Christ who strengthens me"* (Philippians 4:13). My faith had a positive sense of a good outcome.

Fear is a negative emotion based on an expectation of bad things to come. It is rooted in anxiety and a lack of trust in God's fatherly protection and love. But *"Perfect love casts out fear"* (1 John 4:18). God is perfect love. Therefore, by seeking God, His presence and the fullness of His Spirit, we will be set free from fear. When we are conscious of God's power it is very easy to be courageous and bold. We expect success when we are full of God's Spirit and know that we are doing what He is telling us to do. To overcome fear we must look to God and not to natural considerations which could cause our failure if God were not with us. Peter, looking to the wind and the waves, was overcome by a fear which paralyzed his faith and caused him to sink. He needed to keep looking to Jesus. God says,

> *"Fear not, **for I am with you.**"*
>
> (ISAIAH 43:5 emphasis added)

ENEMY NUMBER 4: DISCOURAGEMENT

The final enemy of faith is *discouragement*.

Sometimes we feel discouraged because of physical or emotional weakness, or just plain tiredness. We may be disappointed by the behavior of other Christians. We may be discouraged by persecution from others, even from family members. Perhaps we have waited a long time for what may or may not be God's promise to us, and we have grown impatient?

Most Christians at some time in their life will feel disappointed with God, usually because of a misunderstanding on our part. But Satan wants to use our discouragement to weaken and, if possible, destroy our faith. To overcome discouragement we must make a decision to be strong in the Lord (Hebrews 12:12; Ephesians 6:10). We must want to be strong and stop making excuses for our weakness and failure. We must consider God's faithfulness to us in the past, even through difficulties (Hebrews 10:32–34). We must rededicate ourselves to God's Word, to thankfulness, to prayer, and to the voice of the Spirit. We need to learn to obey the Holy Spirit in small things.

Sometimes even great men of God like Elijah were discouraged. Once, even after a great victory, he ran away from Jezebel, the witch. God restored Elijah through the ministry of angels, through His voice, and by getting him occupied in new missions for Him, full of the promise of hope.

What decisions do you have to make today to become a person of faith and bring success to your future? Have faith that is courageous enough to decide, and your faith will create a positive expectation of a good outcome.

CHAPTER 5

THE
KNOWLEDGE
OF FAITH

Sir Isaac Newton, after his sublime discoveries in science, said, "I do not know what I may appear to the world, but to myself I seem to have only been like a boy playing on the seashore, diverting myself in now and then finding a smoother pebble or a prettier shell than ordinary, whilst the great ocean of truth lay all undiscovered before me." Newton, like many, realized that there are undiscovered truths waiting in the ocean of faith.

There are things in this world that go beyond human reasoning. And equally, there are things is this world that people don't want to acknowledge. For example, scientists don't want to acknowledge that such things as "faith" and "God" exist. They claim that they need to have scientific proof in order to believe either exists.

Today society is full of skepticism and ignorance when it comes to the subject of faith. Faith is believing and trusting in the character of God. It is having the confidence and knowledge that God is on your side. Faith is something we can't touch, smell, taste, hear, or see. We have to believe in our hearts that God exists because the Bible tells us so and because the Holy Spirit within us testifies to the fact of His existence. There will never be any scientific evidence that proves God exists and that faith in Him is valid, because the source of our faith is supernatural and exists outside the realm of science. The source of our faith is found in the Word of God, the Bible. Faith is gained through a knowledge of the Word; knowledge is gained through reading and believing what the Word of God says about our faith. In order to have faith we have to have knowledge!

Someone once said that "knowledge is power". The type of knowledge they were referring to was earthly in nature; it was only head knowledge. But the type of knowledge that the Word of God imparts is a powerful heart-knowledge that will fully equip us for the future.

I meet on a regular basis with a group of young men I call my "mentor group". The group is made up of ten guys who come from various backgrounds. I share with them on a weekly basis the things I have learned about putting faith into action. I'm also constantly telling them to read and learn about other men and women of faith and to gather knowledge where possible.

Ultimately, insight into the life of faith can only come by having acquired the knowledge of God's Word. The Bible says,

> *"My people are destroyed for lack of knowledge.*
> *Because you have rejected knowledge,*
> *I also will reject you from being priest for Me;*
> *Because you have forgotten the law of your God,*
> *I also will forget your children."*

(HOSEA 4:6)

Ignorance is not always bliss!

When I was a kid, grown-ups would often say, "Eat your carrots, they'll make you see better at night!" The story originated from the Second World War. Our bombers were incredibly accurate and were able to make precision attacks on the enemy. This was possible because of the development of radar. The Germans sought to find out how such precision was possible, so the British put out a rumor that all pilots ate a lot of carrots! Imagine that! Hence the saying was born.

But just as many people across the UK believed when they were kids that eating carrots would help them see better at night, so we tend to believe the seemingly "plausible" things that others tell us about faith – unless, that is, we seek out the truth for ourselves.

Make sure therefore, that you are not misinformed. Always seek to expand your knowledge of God's Word because that's what will feed your faith. Faith-knowledge is an important part of your future success. Sadly many Christians have little knowledge of God's Word and this can only result in "little" faith. But that's like having a car with no petrol! It just won't take you anywhere. Your capacity for faith is determined by your knowledge of His Word. The Word is the oxygen that breathes life into your faith.

Never underestimate the knowledge of faith. Faith is able to see what others cannot and perform what some call impossible.

Remember that,

"Faith is the substance of things hoped for, the evidence of things not seen."

(HEBREWS 11:1)

So many times I have faced challenging circumstances and my resolve has been to stand on God's Word. The situation may seem impossible, but the Word of faith says *"I can do all things."* It's a choice of trusting in His promises and not just sitting in the premises!

CHAPTER 6

THE
CONVICTION
OF FAITH

"Never give in – never, never, never, never,
in nothing great or small, large or petty,
never give in except to convictions of honour
and good sense. Never yield to force;
never yield to the apparently overwhelming
might of the enemy."
(Sir Winston Churchill [1874–1965]
in a speech to Harrow School in 1941)

There are basically two kinds of people in the world: those who live by *conviction* and those who live by *convenience*. A man or woman of conviction lives by standards that are not changed by the opinions of others. A man or woman who lives by convenience does what suits them at the time.

A word study shows that,

- *Conviction* = a state of being convinced, to do what is right regardless of the cost.
- *Convenience* = suitability, requiring no effort and conducive to our present state of thinking.

CONVENIENCE WILL CAUSE YOU TO FAIL

There are times in all our lives when we are faced with making decisions based on convenience. Making changes, for example, may cause confrontation or conflict. Often it is easier to go along with the program! But this is not how success is gained. Having a firm conviction about your future goals and destiny is imperative, and if changes and adjustments need to be made in order for you to achieve those goals, then you must have the conviction to follow through. I know a certain gentleman who always agrees with the last person he spoke to – even if the guy before advised him to do the very opposite! Be a person of decision and conviction, not of convenience.

CONVENIENCE WILL CAUSE YOU TO COMPROMISE

Maybe you started out pursuing your God-given dreams all fired up and full of enthusiasm to succeed, but for convenience' sake you compromised, and now you have lost your passion? You *can* get it back, but you will need to make some right choices and then not look back.

"Convenient" people who compromise can lose more than they thought they'd gained. If you lose your convictions due to convenience, then you will lose your power. Conviction is to live on a higher level and to do what is right regardless of the cost, whereas convenience takes no effort and does what suits at the present time.

Now let's turn our attention to a person of conviction:

The Bible says that, *"As* [a man] *thinks in his heart, so is he"* (Proverbs 23:7). You become a product of your convictions. What you believe about yourself and your future, when established as a sure conviction, will determine your success in life. I have no doubt in my mind, having come from a working class family with very little in the way of achievements, that I can and will be a success story.

But how do we become people of conviction?

Our choice often is determined by our feelings, but conviction is not a feeling – we become people of conviction by belief – belief in your future, your destiny, and your success.

Belief in your own future and success is key to producing results. The "law of belief" is nothing new. The "law of belief" states that whatever you believe with your emotions becomes your reality. The "law of belief" says that you do not necessarily believe what you see, but you see what you have already decided to believe.

Your beliefs control your reality. You always act in a manner consistent with your innermost beliefs and convictions. In fact, you can tell what anyone believes simply by looking at what they do. It is not what a person says, or hopes, or writes, or wishes, or intends, that is a clear indication of his or her beliefs – only their actions! It is what a person actually *does* that tells you what he or she truly believes.

This human "law of belief" is reversible fortunately. Since you act in a manner consistent with your beliefs, and you can control your actions, if you engage in actions consistent with the beliefs you desire to hold about yourself and your life, you will eventually develop those beliefs, just as you develop muscles by lifting weights.

For example, if you absolutely believe that you are destined to be a great success in your field of selling, and you walk, talk, act, and behave every single day exactly the way a hugely successful sales person would act, you will eventually develop the mindset of a high performer in selling. As you develop the mindset, you will begin to get the results, and your beliefs will become a fact.

Here are two things you can do immediately to put these ideas into action:

- Begin to believe today that you are programmed and designed to be a big success in your field. Create in yourself the beliefs you most desire – the beliefs that serve you the best.
- Make a habit of walking, talking and behaving as if you were already the big success you imagine yourself to be. Your behavior will build your belief system and will become your reality.

CHAPTER 7

THE FAITH TO PUSH THROUGH

It's true that we will all face resistance in our lives as we expand and develop our faith. Some of the things that resist the expansion of our faith are contentment, fear, and a lack of confidence.

But consider this: the flight of an eagle and the heights it is able to reach are determined by resistance. Resistance can hinder your progress, but it can also be turned around to help you achieve your destiny, depending on your attitude towards it.

When faced with issues that hinder our progress, we need to push through. I've identified three areas that will help and inspire you to fulfill your dream:

DETERMINATION

After the deliverance at Dunkirk, Churchill rallied Britain with his most memorable speech:

> "We shall fight on the beaches, we shall fight on the landing grounds, we shall fight in the fields and in the streets, we shall fight in the hills. We shall never surrender."

"We shall never surrender" should be our attitude when confronted with an excuse to give up and throw the towel in.

In the end determination is what carries you towards your goals.

If there is one gift that you can give to yourself to achieve success in life, it is the power of determination. Without it you are merely a passive spectator in the theatre of life. Those with no determination usually stand on the sideline of life in awe of those who have it. If you have the determination to achieve your dream, nothing can stop you and nothing can deter you.

Hindrances may come and delay your progress, may disturb you temporarily, may even lead you astray for some time, but they cannot withstand the sustained pressure and energy of strong determination – the power that you generate within yourself to hold on to your dreams and to stay the course.

This is one of the most valuable assets you can have in your life. If you have this, you will have everything you want in your life. You will be successful or unsuccessful to the extent that you are determined and committed to your goals.

The dictionary explains determination as "great firmness in carrying out a purpose". Every human being has this characteristic of determination running through their DNA. However, there must be a vision for determination to be birthed. Nearly every story of success in life and business has at its foundation a vision.

What is your vision in life?

Do you dream about being successful? Have you ever seen yourself living in your success? You must have a vision of your success. That vision will give birth to the determination inside of you to push through and see results.

COURAGE

Nearly all of us will face discouraging words from people around us at one time or another. When his commander ordered his decimated squadron to withdraw from the Battle of Copenhagen, Admiral Nelson clapped a telescope to his blind eye, exclaiming: "I really do not see the signal!" He ended, of course, by winning the battle.

Likewise, you must learn to turn a blind eye to your discouragement. It will help if you make a choice to develop and cultivate relationships with winners and achievers, rather than people who constantly surround you with negativity.

Having Faith in
Your God-given Abilities

We are too quick to underestimate the potential that is in us, maybe because of past failure or the words of others. Having a belief in your own ability is essential to your success. If you knew you could not fail, what would you attempt to do? Then do it!

Whether your dream involves creating a company or a product, is about finance, health, improving your home life – or whatever – the chances are you need to take a look at what beliefs currently surround you. Think of your beliefs as part of your plan for success. Beliefs can underpin that plan and make it possible, or they can trip you up and kick you when you're down. Taking a "belief check" from time to time is essential.

Decide which of the beliefs you hold are actually supporting and assisting you. They can stay, but the rest must go! Your beliefs are not an unassailable cerebral list etched in stone that cannot be changed, they are fluid. They can be taken up, put aside, and changed at any time, in order to come into line with your God-given destiny and goals.

Take an inventory today of the beliefs that you hold about yourself, your abilities, your God-given talents, and your future destiny in God. Of those beliefs, which ones should you keep and which should be left behind? In what way are your current beliefs serving you in reaching your God-given destiny? Everybody believes something! So why not choose to believe above the norm and think of yourself as a winner?

Each time I stand up to speak to an audience, whether

there happens to be a few people or thousands, I believe that I'm worth listening to. That's not arrogance, but a confident belief in my own ability.

The beliefs we have about ourselves are responsible for who we ultimately become and what we eventually achieve in life. A positive self-belief is a prerequisite for achieving anything worthwhile.

If you believe that you will fail, then you will! If you believe that you will succeed, then you will! If you believe you will be rich, you will be rich. If you believe you are destined for poverty, you will never rise above that. It is a fact that you become like the person you think you are and believe you are. You achieve only what you think and believe you are capable of.

I remember a friend who always complained about his lack of opportunity in life. I later found that he had very little self-belief. The door of opportunity often opens to those who are knocking with self-belief!

We have to believe that God has put within us the capability to achieve great things. Without this belief, we would never attempt to do anything about our dreams. What's the point of imagining a better life when we have already convinced ourselves that we are incapable of achieving it?

It's easy to say, "Believe in yourself and you will succeed," but how do you develop a powerful belief in yourself? You have to ask yourself, "What limiting beliefs do I have?" Then work to get rid of them, rather focusing on uplifting and positive beliefs.

There is a popular saying that goes, "You are what you think." It means that we often unconsciously set our own limits on what we can and cannot do, based on our beliefs. When you begin to replace those limited small-minded beliefs, it is amazing how you can suddenly raise your game and are able to achieve so much more than you could before.

I have met many successful people in my time. All of them had one very important thing in common – before they succeeded in any way, they first believed that they could. They valued themselves highly and refused to accept any limitations on their potential.

You must learn to believe in yourself and your capabilities. Your beliefs hold great power. They make up the person you become and will influence what you achieve in life. I want you to start believing that you can do anything you truly put your mind to. If you believe you can, you will go to great lengths to prove yourself right. However, if you believe you can't, you will make no effort and you will fail.

CHAPTER 8

LIVING IN THE REALM OF FAITH

We are called as believers to live a life of faith. The Bible tells us that, *"The just shall live by faith"* (Hebrews 10:38) and *"We walk by faith, not by sight"* (2 Corinthians 5:7).

God wants us to live in a realm that has no earthly constraints. I remember visiting Oral Roberts University and had the privilege of meeting the current principal, Richard Roberts. What struck me was the realm of faith that his father lived in which resulted in building one of the finest universities in the world.

Other great generals of faith have seemed to live in a realm that knows no restrictions or limitations. Great men have accomplished great things because of great faith! But living in this realm of faith is not easy. You cannot turn it on like a switch. It is a lifestyle that has been tested. Having come through trials and having overcome impossibilities, faith becomes more than an accessory – it is a necessity. We must live and breathe faith regardless of how things seem, because faith is not shaped by the natural. Rather faith seeks a supernatural outcome.

One day Jesus was standing before a crowd of many thousands. The crowd were hungry and had nothing to eat, and then Jesus was introduced to a young boy with a few loaves and fishes. The disciples looked on in amazement as what seemed to be an impossible feeding challenge became a reality. They were thinking in the natural, but Jesus was living in the realm of faith.

The Christian life was never meant to be lived in an "average" kind of way. We are all called to live in the realm of faith. Our health, wealth, relationships and careers are important, but the pursuit of each of these things with just our own ability is not enough, we need faith.

For many years I struggled with the message of faith, but have since realized that God is pleased with acts of faith.

"Without faith it is impossible to please him."

(HEBREWS 11:6)

Our desire should be to live in the realm of faith and experience that abundant life Christ promised: "I have come to give you life more abundantly" (see John 10:10).

Martin Luther defined faith as "a living, daring confidence in God's grace". It is such an important element that we refer to our walk with God as "the life of faith" and we refer to our beliefs as "the faith". Faith goes well beyond mental beliefs and ideas. Luther said, it is "living, daring". More than a "head thing", it is a "heart thing" and "will thing".

We do not need to be "giants of the faith" to please God. Even a little faith is a powerful thing and small faith can always grow!

> *"I assure you, even if you had faith as small as a mustard seed you could say to this mountain, 'Move from here to there,' and it would move. Nothing would be impossible."*
>
> (MATTHEW 17:20 NLT)

In James 2:14–20 we read James' strong urging that faith must *always* be rooted in action:

> *"Dear brothers and sisters, what's the use of saying you have faith if you don't prove it by your actions? That kind of faith can't save anyone. Suppose you see a brother or sister who needs food or clothing, and you say, 'Well, good-bye and God bless you; stay warm and eat well" – but then you don't give that person any food or clothing. What good does that do? So you see, it isn't enough just to have faith. Faith that doesn't show itself by good deeds is no faith at all – it is dead and useless. Now someone may argue, 'Some people have faith; others have good deeds.' I say, 'I can't see your faith if you don't have good deeds, but I will show you my faith through my good deeds.' Do you still think it's enough just to believe that there is one God? Well, even the*

demons believe this, and they tremble in terror! Fool! When will
you ever learn that faith that does not result in good deeds is
useless?"

(JAMES 2:14–20 NLT)

When you live in the realm of faith there are benefits.
The Bible teaches us that genuine faith is *"more precious than*
gold that perishes" (1 Peter 1:7). Indeed such faith is going to
be *"tested by fire"*. You can expect difficulties and persecution
in your life of faith as well as blessing. Therefore, to
encourage you to hold onto and develop your faith, we will
consider some of the benefits of faith:

FAITH WILL ...

... *bring you salvation*
Faith brings all the benefits of salvation into our lives
including healing, prosperity, peace, love, joy (1 Peter 1:8),
deliverance from demons and curses, sanctification of the
mind and emotions and many other benefits that the Word
of God promises to us.

> *"For by grace you have been saved through faith, and that not of*
> *yourselves; it is the gift of God, not of works, lest anyone should*
> *boast."*
>
> (EPHESIANS 2:8–9)

> *"For God so loved the world that He gave His only begotten*
> *Son, that whoever believes in Him should not perish but have*
> *everlasting life."*
>
> (JOHN 3:16)

"Most assuredly, I say to you, he who hears My word and believes in Him who sent Me has everlasting life, and shall not come into judgment, but has passed from death into life."

(JOHN 5:24)

"For in it the righteousness of God is revealed from faith to faith; as it is written, 'The just shall live by faith.'"

(ROMANS 1:17)

... bring answers to prayer

"And whatever things you ask in prayer, believing, you will receive."

(MATTHEW 21:22)

Since God tells us to pray for our daily bread (Matthew 6:11), faith is therefore a key to our material provision.

... cause your ministry to be effective

Faith is the spiritual force through which our ministry for Christ becomes effective (Mark 11:23; Matthew 17:19–20). Faith is a major key to ministry success. It brings to you what you need for your ministry, and by imparting it to others through your life and your ministry of God's Word, you enable them to receive the blessings of God's grace mentioned above.

Faith is the major key for an effective healing and deliverance ministry. Jesus Christ *"the same yesterday, today, and forever"* (Hebrews 13:8), lives inside the Christian (see Galatians 2:20), and through every believer wants to reveal the power of salvation to men in a way they can see and feel. Through faith, our evangelism for the kingdom of God will not be mere talk, but power (1 Corinthians 4:20).

CHAPTER 9

FAITH MOVES MOUNTAINS

"Jesus answered and said to them, 'Have faith in God. For assuredly, I say to you, whoever says to this mountain, "Be removed and be cast into the sea," and does not doubt in his heart, but believes that those things he says will be done, he will have whatever he says. Therefore I say to you, whatever things you ask when you pray, believe that you receive them, and you will have them.'"
(MARK 11:22–24)

These words of Christ show us that we can move the obstacles that stand before us. Faith does not live in denial of problems, but it speaks out and creates a pathway to victory.

A friend of mine who is a very successful businessman, once shared with me his amazing story:

He started with nothing and having been raised in a working class family he left home with just five pounds in his pocket. But he knew God was calling him to be successful and refused to allow his present circumstances to decide his destiny.

After many years of working hard and standing in faith he and his wife managed to build thirty-three nursing homes and a hospital. He later sold the nursing homes, making him a millionaire. His story is one of faith, and he certainly had mountains to move!

Great acts of mountain-moving faith are also recorded in the Old Testament. Moses was able to get God's people out of Egypt and the slavery they had long endured. As they fled captivity, they were chased by the Egyptians until they came to a seemingly insurmountable obstacle – the Red Sea. Moses however, took his staff, raised it in the air and said, *"see the salvation of the LORD!"* (Exodus 14:13). The Red Sea parted and they crossed on dry land! This was not a stream as some would like to suggest but a *sea*! Similarly, whatever oceans are before you, whatever mountains stand in your way, realize that you can overcome with the confession of faith.

When David stood before the giant Philistine Goliath he faced what seemed like ridiculous odds. He could have fallen prey to the same fear that paralyzed his brothers, but he did not. He allowed faith to rise within his spirit and his confession of faith said, "This Goliath is too big to miss!"

What problems are standing in front of you today, that by their sheer size are demanding you fear them? Allow faith to rise within you and realize that God's power working through you is greater than any giant before you. We all have giants in our lives, but they are there to be conquered, not feared.

Maybe your giant is a fear of the future? God's Word tells us that, "He knows the plans He has for us" (see Jeremiah 29:11 NIV).

You have to allow your faith to trust and believe what God says about your future and nothing else. My future does not lie in the hands of any man, but God! You must not allow present circumstances to determine your future.

Once we held a tent crusade in our town and all the circumstances pointed to a disaster! We pitched the tent on a field in the middle of a housing estate and it rained and rained. In fact, I've never seen so much rain in all my life! I kept hearing the enemy say things like, "Look at this rain! Nobody will come here tonight, especially unbelievers." On top of that, the petrol generator that provided electricity was pouring fumes into the tent and the noise was unbearable. The worship team began and as we praised and worshiped God people began pouring in. To say they were soaked was an understatement!

As I stood up to preach the tent was packed to capacity, with rain hitting the tent so hard it sounded like a bomb raid! The generator made so much noise that even with the PA system I was battling against it! Even as I preached the Gospel I could hear the enemy whispering, "How do you expect people to get saved in this?" He was laughing in my ear. I kept preaching and believing that the Word would accomplish what it was sent forth to do.

After concluding my sermon I asked everyone to bow their heads in prayer. I then invited people to give their lives to Christ by praying with me and to make a public confession by walking to the front.

While the enemy kept whispering "no one will respond" I stood in faith and expected. I realized that night that faith has expectancy and expectancy is an invitation for God to work. I gave the appeal and before I knew it, the front of the tent was full of people making commitments. Every night following many more kept coming and the campaign was a success.

I learnt a valuable lesson during that crusade – that no matter what it looks like on the surface or how impossible things seem, faith always has the final say! The conditions in that tent were far removed from any other outreach I had been in. We had no soft lighting, big plasma screens or gentle choir swaying in the background. What we did have was a tent full of soaking people, choking with petrol fumes, and a generator that gave out more noise than an airplane! But while the enemy was whispering doubt and unbelief the Word of faith prevailed.

My faith spoke to the mountain (Mark 11:22). Even though unbelief tried to fill my mind I shut the door to thoughts of doubt.

I remember one time I took my car to an automatic carwash. As I pulled in, I realized I had forgotten to close the passenger window properly. The carwash began and water gushed through a small opening, leaving me and the inside of the car drenched. The devil works in the same way!

If we allow him entry into our minds with thoughts of unbelief, he will soon flood our lives with destructive doubt. So when Satan comes in and attempts to fill your mind with doubt and unbelief, shut him out!

CHAPTER 10

GREAT FAITH

"A little faith will bring your soul to heaven;
a great faith will bring heaven to your soul."
(Spurgeon)

Matthew chapter 8 tells the story of a man whom Jesus described as having *"great faith"*. We read that,

"When Jesus had entered Capernaum, a centurion came to Him, pleading with Him, saying, 'Lord, my servant is lying at home paralyzed, dreadfully tormented.' And Jesus said to him, 'I will come and heal him.' The centurion answered and said, 'Lord, I am not worthy that You should come under my roof. But only speak a word, and my servant will be healed. For I also

am a man under authority, having soldiers under me. And I say
to this one, "Go," and he goes; and to another, "Come," and he
comes; and to my servant, "Do this," and he does it.' When
Jesus heard it, He marveled, and said to those who followed,
'Assuredly, I say to you, I have not found such great faith, not
even in Israel!'"

(MATTHEW 8:5–10)

The story of the believing centurion is probably the best
example of great faith in the New Testament. Jesus was so
impressed with the centurion's faith that He remarked He
had never found such great faith, even in Israel. It would be
natural to think that such faith should have emerged from
one of the religious leaders of the day, such as the Scribes or
Pharisees, because they were raised and trained in the
Scriptures. This man was just a soldier in the Roman army,
whose military occupation of Palestine was viewed with
disdain by the Jews.

Ironic as it may seem, it isn't always the religious leaders,
ministers, or theologians who aspire to great spiritual things.
Often, it is the unsuspecting people, the housewife, the
plumber, the soldier, or other humble, "ordinary" people
who demonstrate great faith in God. We must never lose
sight of the fact that the gospel is a simple message which is
no respecter of persons. Nor does it require any special
credentials to believe it. The legacy of the centurion is
recorded without the benefit of his name, but his rank of
centurion tells us that he was an officer with authority over
100 men.

He was probably already a believer when he approached
Jesus, since he expressed a comprehension of Christ's

authority and identity (Matthew 8:8–9). It is even more interesting to note that at no time did the centurion actually *ask* Jesus to *heal his servant*. He came to the Lord with a sad report of his servant's suffering, but stopped short of making any request for healing. Perhaps he was hesitant about how Jesus might respond to the request of a non-Jew, especially since he was a soldier in the unpopular army of Rome? Or maybe he wondered whether Jesus would even consider taking the time to help a mere servant? Yet, without hesitation, Jesus voluntarily offered to the centurion, *"I will come and heal him."*

At this point there was no longer any question that it was God's will to heal the servant. Not only was Jesus willing, but by His own suggestion, was ready to go out of His way to the centurion's home to perform the healing. What encouragement this must have been, to sense Jesus' compassion, to witness His eagerness to bring relief and healing to a poor sick soul of low estate.

The centurion's humble, confident response to all this was most remarkable. In essence he said, "Lord, I'm unworthy to have You as a guest in my home, but because I am a man with authority and am acquainted with giving orders to others, I understand Your authority, and know that all You have to do is speak Your word and my servant will be healed" (Matthew 8:5–10).

From the account of the centurion, there are four important principles which we learn about great faith:

► *Great faith begins by being a follower of Christ.*
This means knowing Him personally, and realizing His divine authority. It is obvious that the centurion came to

Jesus with an unusual perception of Christ's position and authority. It is likely that he had been an observer and a follower of Jesus for some time. This indicates that the first step toward a faith which results in answered prayers, is to be a follower of Jesus Christ. We must have a proper relationship with Him, which enables us to approach God with the confidence that our heart is surrendered to the purpose of His will. Not only as our Savior, but as Lord, our beloved Master, whom we follow and serve with all our heart, endeavoring to keep His commandments and do those things which are pleasing to Him. As the scripture says,

> *"Beloved, if our heart does not condemn us, we have confidence toward God. And whatever we ask we receive from Him, because we keep His commandments and do those things that are pleasing in His sight."*

(1 JOHN 3:21–22)

▶ *The motives of great faith are pure, and are in harmony with the will of God.*

The centurion boldly brought his need to Jesus to find out what His will was concerning the afflicted servant. He was not presumptuous or demanding, but reverent and submissive. As for his motive, his concern was not for himself, but the suffering and need of someone else – in fact, a mere servant. Servants were considered the lowest class of people.

It is necessary that we ascertain the will of God in respect to our desires and requests. The Scriptures clearly indicate that God answers those prayers which are in accordance with His will, not just our own will. To have faith's assurance for the desired results of our prayers, our requests must be based upon the criteria of God's wants and desires. Prayer should not be viewed as merely a way to obtain our wishes, but a means that God uses to bring about His own desires. The Bible says,

> *"Now this is the confidence that we have in Him, that if we ask anything according to His will, He hears us. And if we know that He hears us, whatever we ask, we know that we have the petitions that we have asked of Him."*
>
> (1 JOHN 5:14–15)

God's will is revealed through the record of His Word to us, the Bible. We can possess faith for anything promised to us in God's Word, and if we want God's provisions, it is necessary for us to bring our needs to Him. James says that,

> *"We do not have because we do not ask."*
>
> (JAMES 4:2)

But, he also warned that some prayers will go unanswered because of improper motives:

> *"You ask and do not receive, because you ask amiss, that you may spend it on your pleasures."*
>
> (JAMES 4:3)

In fact, one of the major reasons for ineffectual prayer is our tendency towards selfishness. Carnal, self-willed, fleshly desires often drive our prayer requests. Are most of our

requests based upon our own selfish interests? Material
"wants"? Or, is our faith directed toward winning lost souls
to Christ, praying for the sick and afflicted, or the needs of
the poor and homeless? Our motives in relationship with
God's will must be major considerations in our faith.

▶ *Great faith has a humble heart.*
There was no doubt of the sincere humility of the centurion
and his apparent high esteem and honor for the person of
Jesus. He confessed his unworthiness for Jesus to even
come into his home.

But, the Bible says that, *"God resists the proud, but gives grace
to the humble"* (James 4:6). The word "humble" means self-
abasement. We are totally dependent upon God, His mercy
and His strength. What God does for us, in response to our
requests, is not because we have earned or deserve anything.
God acts on our behalf because of His love and grace
(unmerited favor) which comes to us through the redemp-
tion of Jesus Christ. He tells us that when we are in need to
come unto the throne of His grace that we might find help.
In Hebrews we read,

> *"Let us therefore come boldly to the throne of grace, that we may
> obtain mercy and find grace to help in time of need."*
>
> (HEBREWS 4:16)

▶ *Great faith has a complete trust in the dependability
   of God's Word, and accepts it as fact above any other
   evidence or circumstance.*
The centurion was so thoroughly convinced of the authority of Christ's word that He did not find it necessary for

Jesus to personally visit his servant. He felt assured that if Christ would only give the command, then His servant would be healed. He didn't need to "see" anything or "feel" anything, but was willing to rest solely upon God's word to him.

Such were the characteristics of Abraham's faith, who believed God's word of promise, even though all natural circumstances were against him and there were no signs of the promise for seventeen years:

> *"He did not waver at the promise of God through unbelief, but was strengthened in faith, giving glory to God, and being fully convinced that what He had promised He was also able to perform."*

> (ROMANS 4:20–21)

God's Word is the very basis of our faith. His Word is the source of all creation, and nothing can withstand its power or force. His Word is absolutely trustworthy, in fact more trustworthy than the things of this world, which we can see or perceive with our senses. Each of us then, must have total confidence in the fact that what God has said to us will indeed come to pass – despite evidence that seems to suggest otherwise.

May God encourage you to follow these principles of great faith!

CHAPTER 11

HOW TO DEVELOP YOUR FAITH

We have seen how important faith is. Yet some people despair, thinking that they don't have faith. Yet faith is God's gift to us and faith can increase, grow and develop as we immerse ourselves in God's Word (Romans 10:17). If you are not full of faith today, that doesn't mean you will be that way all your life. You can choose to be a person of faith!

Here are some keys to developing faith:

▶ *Listen to the Word of God as much as possible.*

"Faith comes by hearing, and hearing by the word of God."
(ROMANS 10:17)

Constant attention to the Word of God produces faith, especially if we attend to it with an open heart and mind. The book of Proverbs encourages us to constantly keep the Word in our hearts and to keep our attention on it (Proverbs 4:20–22).

What we listen to affects what we believe. If we listen to the TV more than to the Word of God, then we will believe the lies of the world more than we will believe what God says. Constant attention to lies produces deception. Eventually the mind will accept something, if that thing is heard often enough and is allowed to persuade us. That is why we should keep hearing the Word of God, through preaching, Christian tapes, confession of the Word, daily fellowship with godly Christians etc. This will cause us to store up truth in our hearts.

▶ *Realize that every believer has been given a measure of faith by God* (Romans 12:3).
All of us have faith, of that there is no question. We just have to use and develop what God has given us. We must put it into action.

▶ *Pray in tongues and be full of the Spirit* (Jude 20).
If you have been baptized in the Spirit as the disciples were in the book of Acts, you should pray and praise in tongues often, because through this you "edify yourself"

(1 Corinthians 14:4) and "build yourself up in your most holy faith". Praying in tongues is one key to being full of the Spirit.

▶ *Obey God and the conviction of the Holy Spirit.*
It is as you practice the walk of faith that you gain strength. God will not reveal greater things to you until you are faithful in the things He is showing you *now*. Therefore, continued obedience to the Spirit and what He is showing you through the Word or through your conscience is important in the development of your faith. You cannot have living faith without taking some practical steps of obedience. Act on what God is saying!

▶ *Give thanks.*
Give thanks for the results of your prayers in God's will, even before you see them. Don't complain – that shows you doubt God's love and God's answer to your situation. Give thanks in all situations (1 Thessalonians 5:18).

▶ *Develop a life of praise and worship.*
Praise drives the powers of darkness away and brings the throne of God into your circumstances. Praising God is an act of faith and helps your faith to grow. It is commanded (Hebrews 13:15). Worship is admiring God through the Spirit. If you can perceive who God is, His power, faithfulness and love, your trust and faith in Him will grow.

▶ *Spend as much time as you can with people of faith.*
It will help you to spend time around those who are living a faith-filled life and can stretch and challenge your own

experience of faith-in-action. The spirit of faith on them will touch your life and inspire you to press on (Proverbs 13:20).

▶ *Speak the Word.*
By speaking God's Word out loud, you exercise your faith. When you hear God's Word declared, even from your own lips, it can build you up and store up truth within you. God's Word is anointed and alive; it has the power when it is spoken out, to change the spiritual atmosphere (Joshua 1:8; Romans 10:10). Confession of God's Word (saying the same thing as God's Word) brings you into a place where the Lord will move to fulfill it (Hebrews 3:1).

▶ *Seek holiness and purity of heart.*
The writer of Hebrews instructs us to, *"Pursue peace with all men, and holiness, without which no one will see the Lord"* (Hebrews 12:14). It is with the heart that man believes (Romans 10:10). To the extent that our hearts have uncleanness, unforgiveness and other bad conditions within, we lose the spiritual "senses" or perceptions which enable our hearts to believe – whereas purity and faith feed each other.

▶ *Remember that faith works by love* (Galatians 5:6).
The centurion (Matthew 8:5–13) and the woman of Canaan (Matthew 15:21–28) were both motivated by their love for another in coming to Jesus. Both were described as having great faith. Let us believe God for others to be blessed, in a spirit of love, and as we give of ourselves God will give blessings to us also (Luke 6:37). This is related to the idea of "seed-faith". You express your faith by "planting a seed".

This may be through some form of giving to others. God will release a multiplied harvest in return if we endure and do not faint (Hebrews 10:36).

What We Say
And
What God Says

I hope this book has brought you hope and inspiration for living a faith-filled life. In the following pages I have gathered together many scriptures about faith for you to pray through and mediate on. As I conclude, I want you also to think about the statements below. Often our view of things and God's view of things do not match up and we tend to make negative declarations on the basis of "our perspective". But, how does God view you, your life, the circumstances you currently find yourself in? As an exercise, try reading out loud God's response to the things we commonly say.

You say: "It's impossible"
God says: "All things are possible" (Luke 18:27)

You say: "I'm too tired"
God says: "I will give you rest" (Matthew 11:28–30)

You say: "Nobody really loves me"
God says: "I love you" (John 3:16 and John 13:34)

You say: "I can't go on"
God says: "My grace is sufficient" (2 Corinthians
              12:9 and Psalm 91:15)

You say: "I can't figure things out"
God says: "I will direct your steps" (Proverbs 3:5–6)

You say: "I can't do it"
God says: "You can do all things through Christ"
              (Philippians 4:13)

You say: "I'm not able"
God says: "I am able" (2 Corinthians 9:8)

You say: "It's not worth it"
God says: "It will be worth it" (Romans 8:28)

You say: "I can't forgive myself"
God says: "I ***forgive you***" (1 John 1:9 and
              Romans 8:1)

You say: "I can't manage"
God says: "I will supply all your needs" (Philippians
              4:19)

You say: "I'm afraid"
God says: "I have not given you a spirit of fear"
              (2 Timothy 1:7)

You say: "I'm always worried and frustrated"

God says: "Cast all your cares on **Me**" (1 Peter 5:7)

You say: "I don't have enough faith"

God says: "I've given everyone a measure of faith"
              (Romans 12:3)

You say: "I'm not smart enough"

God says: "I give you wisdom" (1 Corinthians 1:30)

You say: "I feel all alone"

God says: "I will never leave you or forsake you"
              (Hebrews 13:5)

SCRIPTURES
ON FAITH (KJV)

Note: Text in **_bold italics_** indicates emphasis has been added.

"And he said, I will hide my face from them, I will see what their end shall be: for they are a very froward generation, children in whom is no **_faith._***"*

(DEUTERONOMY 32:20)

"Behold, his soul which is lifted up is not upright in him: **_but the just shall live by his faith._***"*

(HABAKKUK 2:4)

*"Wherefore, if God so clothe the grass of the field, which to day is, and tomorrow is cast into the oven, shall he not much more clothe you, O ye of little **faith**?"*

(MATTHEW 6:30)

*"When Jesus heard it, he marveled, and said to them that followed, Verily I say unto you, I have not found so great **faith**, no, not in Israel."*

(MATTHEW 8:10)

*"And he saith unto them, Why are ye fearful, O ye of little **faith**? Then he arose, and rebuked the winds and the sea; and there was a great calm."*

(MATTHEW 8:26)

*"And, behold, they brought to him a man sick of the palsy, lying on a bed: and Jesus seeing their **faith** said unto the sick of the palsy; Son, be of good cheer; thy sins be forgiven thee."*

(MATTHEW 9:2)

*"But Jesus turned him about, and when he saw her, he said, Daughter, be of good comfort; thy **faith** hath made thee whole. And the woman was made whole from that hour."*

(MATTHEW 9:22)

*"Then touched he their eyes, saying, According to your **faith** be it unto you."*

(MATTHEW 9:29)

*"And immediately Jesus stretched forth his hand, and caught him, and said unto him, O thou of little **faith**, wherefore didst thou doubt?"*

(MATTHEW 14:31)

*"Then Jesus answered and said unto her, O woman, great is thy **faith**: be it unto thee even as thou wilt. And her daughter was made whole from that very hour."*

(MATTHEW 15:28)

*"Which when Jesus perceived, he said unto them, O ye of little **faith**, why reason ye among yourselves, because ye have brought no bread?"*

(MATTHEW 16:8)

*"And Jesus said unto them, Because of your unbelief: for verily I say unto you, If ye have **faith** as a grain of mustard seed, ye shall say unto this mountain, Remove hence to yonder place; and it shall remove; and nothing shall be impossible unto you."*

(MATTHEW 17:20)

*"Jesus answered and said unto them, Verily I say unto you, If ye have **faith**, and doubt not, ye shall not only do this which is done to the fig tree, but also if ye shall say unto this mountain, Be thou removed, and be thou cast into the sea; it shall be done."*

(MATTHEW 21:21)

*"When Jesus saw their **faith**, he said unto the sick of the palsy, Son, thy sins be forgiven thee."*

(MARK 2:5)

*"And he said unto them, Why are ye so fearful? how is it that ye have no **faith**?"*

(MARK 4:40)

*"And he said unto her, Daughter, thy **faith** hath made thee whole; go in peace, and be whole of thy plague."*

(MARK 5:34)

"And Jesus said unto him, Go thy way; thy faith hath made thee whole. And immediately he received his sight, and followed Jesus in the way."

(MARK 10:52)

*"And Jesus answering saith unto them, Have **faith** in God."*

(MARK 11:22)

*"And when he saw their **faith**, he said unto him, Man, thy sins are forgiven thee."*

(LUKE 5:20)

*"When Jesus heard these things, he marveled at him, and turned him about, and said unto the people that followed him, I say unto you, I have not found so great **faith**, no, not in Israel."*

(LUKE 7:9)

*"And he said to the woman, Thy **faith** hath saved thee; go in peace."*

(LUKE 7:50)

*"And he said unto them, Where is your **faith**? And they being afraid wondered, saying one to another, What manner of man is this! for he commandeth even the winds and water, and they obey him."*

(LUKE 8:25)

*"And he said unto her, Daughter, be of good comfort: thy **faith** hath made thee whole; go in peace."*

(LUKE 8:48)

"If then God so clothe the grass, which is to day in the field, and to morrow is cast into the oven; how much more will he clothe you, O ye of little **faith**?" (LUKE 12:28)

"And the apostles said unto the Lord, ***Increase our faith.****"*
(LUKE 17:5)

"And the Lord said, If ye had ***faith*** *as a grain of mustard seed, ye might say unto this sycamine tree, Be thou plucked up by the root, and be thou planted in the sea; and it should obey you."*
(LUKE 17:6)

"And he said unto him, Arise, go thy way: thy ***faith*** *hath made thee whole."*
(LUKE 17:19)

"I tell you that he will avenge them speedily. Nevertheless when the Son of man cometh, shall he find ***faith*** *on the earth?"*
(LUKE 18:8)

"And Jesus said unto him, Receive thy sight: thy ***faith*** *hath saved thee."*
(LUKE 18:42)

"But I have prayed for thee, that thy ***faith*** *fail not: and when thou art converted, strengthen thy brethren."*
(LUKE 22:32)

"And his name through ***faith*** *in his name hath made this man strong, whom ye see and know: yea, the* ***faith*** *which is by him hath given him this perfect soundness in the presence of you all."*
(ACTS 3:16)

*"And the saying pleased the whole multitude: and they chose Stephen, a man **full of faith** and of the Holy Ghost, and Philip, and Prochorus, and Nicanor, and Timon, and Parmenas, and Nicolas a proselyte of Antioch."*

(ACTS 6:5)

*"And Stephen, full of **faith** and power, did great wonders and miracles among the people."*

(ACTS 6:8)

*"For he was a good man, and full of the Holy Ghost and of **faith**: and much people was added unto the Lord."*

(ACTS 11:24)

*"The same heard Paul speak: who stedfastly beholding him, and perceiving that he had **faith** to be healed"*

(ACTS 14:9)

*"And when they were come, and had gathered the church together, they rehearsed all that God had done with them, and how he had opened the door of **faith** unto the Gentiles."*

(ACTS 14:27)

*"And put no difference between us and them, purifying their hearts by **faith**."*

(ACTS 15:9)

*"Testifying both to the Jews, and also to the Greeks, repentance toward God, and **faith** toward our Lord Jesus Christ."*

(ACTS 20:21)

*"To open their eyes, and to turn them from darkness to light, and from the power of Satan unto God, that they may receive forgiveness of sins, and inheritance among them which are sanctified by **faith** that is in me."*

(ACTS 26:18)

*"First, I thank my God through Jesus Christ for you all, that your **faith** is spoken of throughout the whole world."*

(ROMANS 1:8)

*"That is, that I may be comforted together with you by the mutual **faith** both of you and me."*

(ROMANS 1:12)

*"For therein is the righteousness of God revealed from **faith to faith**: as it is written, **The just shall live by faith**."*

(ROMANS 1:17)

*"For what if some did not believe? shall their unbelief make the **faith** of God without effect?"*

(ROMANS 3:3)

*"Even the righteousness of God which is **by faith of Jesus Christ** unto all and upon all them that believe: for there is no difference."*

(ROMANS 3:22)

*"Whom God hath set forth to be a propitiation through **faith** in his blood, to declare his righteousness for the remission of sins that are past, through the forbearance of God."*

(ROMANS 3:25)

*"Where is boasting then? It is excluded. By what law? of works? Nay: but by the **law of faith**."*

(ROMANS 3:27)

*"Therefore we conclude that a man is **justified by faith without the deeds of the law**."*

(ROMANS 3:28)

*"Seeing it is one God, which shall justify the circumcision by **faith**, and uncircumcision through **faith**."*

(ROMANS 3:30)

*"Do we then make void the law through **faith**? God forbid: yea, we establish the law."*

(ROMANS 3:31)

*"But to him that worketh not, but believeth on him that justifieth the ungodly, his **faith is counted for righteousness**."*

(ROMANS 4:5)

*"Cometh this blessedness then upon the circumcision only, or upon the uncircumcision also? for we say that **faith** was reckoned to Abraham for righteousness."*

(ROMANS 4:9)

*"And he received the sign of circumcision, a seal of the righteousness of the **faith** which he had yet being uncircumcised: that he might be the father of all them that believe, though they be not circumcised; that righteousness might be imputed unto them also."*

(ROMANS 4:11)

*"And the father of circumcision to them who are not of the circumcision only, but who also walk in the steps of that **faith** of our father Abraham, which he had being yet uncircumcised."*

(ROMANS 4:12)

*"For the promise, that he should be the heir of the world, was not to Abraham, or to his seed, through the law, but through the **righteousness of faith**."*

(ROMANS 4:13)

*"For if they which are of the law be heirs, **faith** is made void, and the promise made of none effect."*

(ROMANS 4:14)

*"Therefore it is of **faith**, that it might be by grace; to the end the promise might be sure to all the seed; not to that only which is of the law, but to that also which is of the **faith** of Abraham; who is the father of us all."*

(ROMANS 4:16)

*"And being not weak in **faith**, he considered not his own body now dead, when he was about an hundred years old, neither yet the deadness of Sara's womb"*

(ROMANS 4:19)

*"He staggered not at the promise of God through unbelief; but was **strong in faith**, giving glory to God."*

(ROMANS 4:20)

*"Therefore being **justified by faith**, we have peace with God through our Lord Jesus Christ."*

(ROMANS 5:1)

*"By whom also we have **access by faith** into this grace wherein we stand, and rejoice in hope of the glory of God."*

(ROMANS 5:2)

*"What shall we say then? That the Gentiles, which followed not after righteousness, have attained to righteousness, even the righteousness which is of **faith**."*

(ROMANS 9:30)

*"Wherefore? Because they sought it not by **faith**, but as it were by the works of the law. For they stumbled at that stumblingstone."*

(ROMANS 9:32)

*"But the righteousness which is of **faith** speaketh on this wise, Say not in thine heart, Who shall ascend into heaven? (that is, to bring Christ down from above)."*

(ROMANS 10:6)

*"But what saith it? The word is nigh thee, even in thy mouth, and in thy heart: that is, the word of **faith**, which we preach."*

(ROMANS 10:8)

*"So then **faith cometh by hearing**, and hearing by the word of God."*

(ROMANS 10:17)

*"Well; because of unbelief they were broken off, and thou standest by **faith**. Be not highminded, but fear."*

(ROMANS 11:20)

"For I say, through the grace given unto me, to every man that is among you, not to think of himself more highly than he ought to think; but to think soberly, according as God hath dealt to every man the **measure of faith**.*"*

(ROMANS 12:3)

"Having then gifts differing according to the grace that is given to us, whether prophecy, let us prophesy according to the proportion of **faith**.*"*

(ROMANS 12:6)

"Him that is weak in the **faith** *receive ye, but not to doubtful disputations."*

(ROMANS 14:1)

"Hast thou **faith**? *have it to thyself before God. Happy is he that condemneth not himself in that thing which he alloweth."*

(ROMANS 14:22)

"And he that doubteth is damned if he eat, because he eateth not of **faith**: *for whatsoever is not of* **faith** *is sin."*

(ROMANS 14:23)

"But now is made manifest, and by the scriptures of the prophets, according to the commandment of the everlasting God, made known to all nations for the obedience of **faith**.*"*

(ROMANS 16:26)

"That your **faith** *should not stand in the wisdom of men, but in the power of God."*

(1 CORINTHIANS 2:5)

*"To another **faith** by the same Spirit; to another the gifts of healing by the same Spirit."*

(1 CORINTHIANS 12:9)

*"And though I have the gift of prophecy, and understand all mysteries, and all knowledge; and though I have all **faith**, so that I could remove mountains, and have not charity, I am nothing."*

(1 CORINTHIANS 13:2)

*"And now abideth **faith**, hope, charity, these three; but the greatest of these is charity."*

(1 CORINTHIANS 13:13)

*"And if Christ be not risen, then is our preaching vain, and your **faith** is also vain."*

(1 CORINTHIANS 15:14)

*"And if Christ be not raised, your **faith** is vain; ye are yet in your sins."*

(1 CORINTHIANS 15:17)

*"Watch ye, stand fast in the **faith**, quit you like men, be strong."*

(1 CORINTHIANS 16:13)

*"Not for that we have dominion over your **faith**, but are helpers of your joy: **for by faith ye stand**."*

(2 CORINTHIANS 1:24)

*"We having the same spirit of **faith**, according as it is written, I believed, and therefore have I spoken; we also believe, and therefore speak."*

(2 CORINTHIANS 4:13)

*"For we walk by **faith**, not by sight."*

(2 CORINTHIANS 5:7)

*"Therefore, as ye abound in every thing, in **faith**, and utterance, and knowledge, and in all diligence, and in your love to us, see that ye abound in this grace also."*

(2 CORINTHIANS 8:7)

*"Not boasting of things without our measure, that is, of other men's labors; but having hope, when your **faith** is increased, that we shall be enlarged by you according to our rule abundantly."*

(2 CORINTHIANS 10:15)

*"Knowing that a man is not justified by the works of the law, **but by the faith of Jesus Christ**, even we have believed in Jesus Christ, that we might be **justified by the faith of Christ**, and not by the works of the law: for by the works of the law shall no flesh be justified."*

(GALATIANS 2:16)

*"I am crucified with Christ: nevertheless I live; yet not I, but Christ liveth in me: and the life which I now live in the flesh I live by the **faith** of the Son of God, who loved me, and gave himself for me."*

(GALATIANS 2:20)

*"This only would I learn of you, Received ye the Spirit by the works of the law, or by the **hearing of faith**?"*

(GALATIANS 3:2)

*"He therefore that ministereth to you the Spirit, and worketh miracles among you, doeth he it by the works of the law, or by the **hearing of faith**?"*

(GALATIANS 3:5)

*"Know ye therefore that they which are of **faith**, the same are the children of Abraham."*

(GALATIANS 3:7)

*"And the scripture, foreseeing that God would justify the **heathen through faith**, preached before the gospel unto Abraham, saying, In thee shall all nations be blessed."*

(GALATIANS 3:8)

*"So then they which be of **faith** are blessed with faithful Abraham."*

(GALATIANS 3:9)

*"But that no man is justified by the law in the sight of God, it is evident: for, The **just shall live by faith**."*

(GALATIANS 3:11)

*"And the law is not of **faith**: but, The man that doeth them shall live in them."*

(GALATIANS 3:12)

*"That the blessing of Abraham might come on the Gentiles through Jesus Christ; that we might receive the promise of the Spirit through **faith**."*

(GALATIANS 3:14)

*"But the scripture hath concluded all under sin, that the promise by **faith** of Jesus Christ might be given to them that believe."*

(GALATIANS 3:22)

*"But before **faith** came, we were kept under the law, shut up unto the **faith** which should afterwards be revealed."*

(GALATIANS 3:23)

*"Wherefore the law was our schoolmaster to bring us unto Christ, that we might be **justified by faith**."*

(GALATIANS 3:24)

*"But after that **faith** is come, we are no longer under a schoolmaster."*

(GALATIANS 3:25)

*"For ye are all the **children of God by faith in Christ Jesus**."*

(GALATIANS 3:26)

*"For we through the Spirit wait for the hope of righteousness **by faith**."*

(GALATIANS 5:5)

*"For in Jesus Christ neither circumcision availeth any thing, nor uncircumcision; but **faith** which worketh by love."*

(GALATIANS 5:6)

*"But the fruit of the Spirit is love, joy, peace, longsuffering, gentleness, goodness, **faith**."*

(GALATIANS 5:22)

*"Wherefore I also, after I heard of your **faith in the Lord Jesus**, and love unto all the saints."*

(EPHESIANS 1:15)

*"For by grace are ye **saved through faith**; and that not of yourselves: it is the gift of God."*

(EPHESIANS 2:8)

*"In whom we have boldness and access with confidence by the **faith** of him."*

(EPHESIANS 3:12)

*"That Christ may dwell in your hearts **by faith**; that ye, being rooted and grounded in love."*

(EPHESIANS 3:17)

*"One Lord, one **faith**, one baptism."*

(EPHESIANS 4:5)

*"Above all, taking the **shield of faith**, wherewith ye shall be able to quench all the fiery darts of the wicked."*

(EPHESIANS 6:16)

*"Peace be to the brethren, and **love with faith**, from God the Father and the Lord Jesus Christ."*

(EPHESIANS 6:23)

*"And be found in him, not having mine own righteousness, which is of the law, but that which is through the **faith of Christ**, the righteousness which is of God **by faith**."*

(PHILIPPIANS 3:9)

*"Since we heard of your **faith in Christ Jesus**, and of the love which ye have to all the saints."*

(COLOSSIANS 1:4)

*"If ye continue in the **faith grounded** and settled, and be not moved away from the hope of the gospel, which ye have heard, and which was*

preached to every creature which is under heaven; whereof I Paul am made a minister."

(COLOSSIANS 1:23)

*"For though I be absent in the flesh, yet am I with you in the spirit, joying and beholding your order, and the stedfastness of your **faith in Christ**."*

(COLOSSIANS 2:5)

*"Rooted and built up in him, and **stablished in the faith**, as ye have been taught, abounding therein with thanksgiving."*

(COLOSSIANS 2:7)

*"Buried with him in baptism, wherein also ye are risen with **him through the faith** of the operation of God, who hath raised him from the dead."*

(COLOSSIANS 2:12)

*"Remembering without ceasing your work of **faith**, and labour of love, and patience of hope in our Lord Jesus Christ, in the sight of God and our Father."*

(1 THESSALONIANS 1:3)

*"For from you sounded out the word of the Lord not only in Macedonia and Achaia, but also in every place your **faith** to God-ward is spread abroad; so that we need not to speak any thing."*

(1 THESSALONIANS 1:8)

*"But now when Timotheus came from you unto us, and brought us good tidings of your **faith** and charity, and that ye have good remembrance of us always, desiring greatly to see us, as we also to see you."*

(1 THESSALONIANS 3:6)

*"Therefore, brethren, we were comforted over you in all our affliction and distress by your **faith**."*

(1 THESSALONIANS 3:7)

*"Night and day praying exceedingly that we might see your face, and might perfect that which is lacking in your **faith**?"*

(1 THESSALONIANS 3:10)

*"But let us, who are of the day, be sober, putting on the breastplate of **faith** and love; and for an helmet, the hope of salvation."*

(1 THESSALONIANS 5:8)

*"We are bound to thank God always for you, brethren, as it is meet, because that your **faith groweth exceedingly**, and the charity of every one of you all toward each other aboundeth."*

(2 THESSALONIANS 1:3)

*"So that we ourselves glory in you in the churches of God for your patience and **faith** in all your persecutions and tribulations that ye endure."*

(2 THESSALONIANS 1:4)

*"Wherefore also we pray always for you, that our God would count you worthy of this calling, and fulfill all the good pleasure of his goodness, and the work of **faith with power**."*

(2 THESSALONIANS 1:11)

*"And that we may be delivered from unreasonable and wicked men: **for all men have not faith**."*

(2 THESSALONIANS 3:2)

*"Neither give heed to fables and endless genealogies, which minister questions, rather than godly edifying which is in **faith**: so do."*

(1 TIMOTHY 1:4)

*"Now the end of the commandment is charity out of a pure heart, and of a good conscience, and of **faith unfeigned**."*

(1 TIMOTHY 1:5)

*"And the grace of our Lord was exceeding **abundant with faith** and love which is in Christ Jesus."*

(1 TIMOTHY 1:14)

*"Holding **faith**, and a good conscience; which some having put away concerning faith have made shipwreck."*

(1 TIMOTHY 1:19)

*"Whereunto I am ordained a preacher, and an apostle, (I speak the truth in Christ, and lie not;) a teacher of the Gentiles in **faith** and verity."*

(1 TIMOTHY 2:7)

*"Notwithstanding she shall be saved in childbearing, if they **continue in faith** and charity and holiness with sobriety."*

(1 TIMOTHY 2:15)

*"Holding the mystery of the **faith in a pure conscience**."*

(1 TIMOTHY 3:9)

*"For they that have used the office of a deacon well purchase to themselves a good degree, and great boldness in the **faith which is in Christ Jesus**."*

(1 TIMOTHY 3:13)

*"Now the Spirit speaketh expressly, that in the latter times some shall depart from the **faith**, giving heed to seducing spirits, and doctrines of devils."*

(1 TIMOTHY 4:1)

*"If thou put the brethren in remembrance of these things, thou shalt be a good minister of Jesus Christ, **nourished up in the words of faith** and of good doctrine, whereunto thou hast attained."*

(1 TIMOTHY 4:6)

*"Let no man despise thy youth; but be thou an example of the believers, in word, in conversation, in charity, in spirit, **in faith**, in purity."*

(1 TIMOTHY 4:12)

*"But if any provide not for his own, and specially for those of his own house, he hath denied the **faith**, and is worse than an infidel."*

(1 TIMOTHY 5:8)

*"Having damnation, because they have cast off their first **faith**."*

(1 TIMOTHY 5:12)

*"For the love of money is the root of all evil: which while some coveted after, they have erred from the **faith**, and pierced themselves through with many sorrows."*

(1 TIMOTHY 6:10)

*"But thou, O man of God, flee these things; and follow after righteousness, godliness, **faith**, love, patience, meekness."*

(1 TIMOTHY 6:11)

*"When I call to remembrance the unfeigned **faith** that is in thee, which dwelt first in thy grandmother Lois, and thy mother Eunice; and I am persuaded that in thee also."*

(2 TIMOTHY 1:5)

*"Hold fast the form of sound words, which thou hast heard of me, **in faith** and love which is in Christ Jesus."*

(2 TIMOTHY 1:13)

*"Who concerning the truth have erred, saying that the resurrection is past already; and overthrow the **faith** of some."*

(2 TIMOTHY 2:18)

*"Flee also youthful lusts: but follow righteousness, **faith**, charity, peace, with them that call on the Lord out of a pure heart."*

(2 TIMOTHY 2:22)

*"But thou hast fully known my doctrine, manner of life, purpose, **faith**, longsuffering, charity, patience."*

(2 TIMOTHY 3:10)

*"And that from a child thou hast known the holy scriptures, which are able to make thee wise unto **salvation through faith which is in Christ Jesus**."*

(2 TIMOTHY 3:15)

*"I have fought a good fight, I have finished my course, I have **kept the faith**."*

(2 TIMOTHY 4:7)

*"Paul, a servant of God, and an apostle of Jesus Christ, according to the **faith** of God's elect, and the acknowledging of the truth which is after godliness."*

(TITUS 1:1)

*"This witness is true. Wherefore rebuke them sharply, that they may be **sound in the faith**."*

(TITUS 1:13)

*"That the aged men be sober, grave, temperate, **sound in faith**, in charity, in patience."*

(TITUS 2:2)

*"Hearing of thy love and **faith**, which thou hast toward the Lord Jesus, and toward all saints."*

(PHILEMON 1:5)

*"That the communication of thy **faith** may become effectual by the acknowledging of every good thing which is in you in Christ Jesus."*

(PHILEMON 1:6)

*"For unto us was the gospel preached, as well as unto them: but the word preached did not profit them, not being mixed with **faith** in them that heard it."*

(HEBREWS 4:2)

*"Therefore leaving the principles of the doctrine of Christ, let us go on unto perfection; not laying again the foundation of repentance from dead works, and of **faith** toward God."*

(HEBREWS 6:1)

*"That ye be not slothful, but followers of them who through **faith** and patience inherit the promises."*

(HEBREWS 6:12)

*"Let us draw near with a true heart in **full assurance of faith**, having our hearts sprinkled from an evil conscience, and our bodies washed with pure water."*

(HEBREWS 10:22)

*"Let us hold fast the profession of our **faith** without wavering; (for he is **faithful** that promised)."*

(HEBREWS 10:23)

*"Now the **just shall live by faith**: but if any man draw back, my soul shall have no pleasure in him."*

(HEBREWS 10:38)

*"Now **faith** is the substance of things hoped for, the evidence of things not seen."*

(HEBREWS 11:1)

*"**Through faith** we understand that the worlds were framed by the word of God, so that things which are seen were not made of things which do appear."*

(HEBREWS 11:3)

*"**By faith** Abel offered unto God a more excellent sacrifice than Cain, by which he obtained witness that he was righteous, God testifying of his gifts: and by it he being dead yet speaketh."*

(HEBREWS 11:4)

*"**By faith** Enoch was translated that he should not see death; and was not found, because God had translated him: for before his translation he had this testimony, that he pleased God."*

(HEBREWS 11:5)

*"But **without faith it is impossible to please him**: for he that cometh to God must believe that he is, and that he is a rewarder of them that diligently seek him."*

(HEBREWS 11:6)

*"**By faith** Noah, being warned of God of things not seen as yet, moved with fear, prepared an ark to the saving of his house; by the which he condemned the world, and became heir of the righteousness which is by **faith**."*

(HEBREWS 11:7)

*"**By faith** Abraham, when he was called to go out into a place which he should after receive for an inheritance, obeyed; and he went out, not knowing whither he went."*

(HEBREWS 11:8)

*"**By faith** he sojourned in the land of promise, as in a strange country, dwelling in tabernacles with Isaac and Jacob, the heirs with him of the same promise."*

(HEBREWS 11:9)

*"**Through faith** also Sara herself received strength to conceive seed, and was delivered of a child when she was past age, because she judged him faithful who had promised."*

(HEBREWS 11:11)

*"These all died in **faith**, not having received the promises, but having seen them afar off, and were persuaded of them, and embraced them, and confessed that they were strangers and pilgrims on the earth."*

(HEBREWS 11:13)

*"**By faith** Abraham, when he was tried, offered up Isaac: and he that had received the promises offered up his only begotten son."*

(HEBREWS 11:17)

*"**By faith** Isaac blessed Jacob and Esau concerning things to come."*

(HEBREWS 11:20)

*"**By faith** Jacob, when he was a dying, blessed both the sons of Joseph; and worshipped, leaning upon the top of his staff."*

(HEBREWS 11:21)

*"**By faith** Joseph, when he died, made mention of the departing of the children of Israel; and gave commandment concerning his bones."*

(HEBREWS 11:22)

*"**By faith** Moses, when he was born, was hid three months of his parents, because they saw he was a proper child; and they were not afraid of the king's commandment."*

(HEBREWS 11:23)

*"**By faith** Moses, when he was come to years, refused to be called the son of Pharaoh's daughter."*

(HEBREWS 11:24)

*"**By faith** he forsook Egypt, not fearing the wrath of the king: for he endured, as seeing him who is invisible."*

(HEBREWS 11:27)

*"**Through faith** he kept the passover, and the sprinkling of blood, lest he that destroyed the firstborn should touch them."*

(HEBREWS 11:28)

*"**By faith** they passed through the Red sea as by dry land: which the Egyptians assaying to do were drowned."*

(HEBREWS 11:29)

*"**By faith** the walls of Jericho fell down, after they were compassed about seven days."*

(HEBREWS 11:30)

*"**By faith** the harlot Rahab perished not with them that believed not, when she had received the spies with peace."*

(HEBREWS 11:31)

*"Who **through faith** subdued kingdoms, wrought righteousness, obtained promises, stopped the mouths of lions."*

(HEBREWS 11:33)

*"And these all, having obtained a good report **through faith**, received not the promise."*

(HEBREWS 11:39)

*"Looking unto Jesus the author and finisher of our **faith**; who for the joy that was set before him endured the cross, despising the shame, and is set down at the right hand of the throne of God."*

(HEBREWS 12:2)

*"Remember them which have the rule over you, who have spoken unto you the word of God: whose **faith** follow, considering the end of their conversation."*

(HEBREWS 13:7)

*"Knowing this, that the trying of **your faith** worketh patience."*

(JAMES 1:3)

*"But let him **ask in faith**, nothing wavering. For he that wavereth is like a wave of the sea driven with the wind and tossed."*

(JAMES 1:6)

*"My brethren, have not the **faith** of our Lord Jesus Christ, the Lord of glory, with respect of persons."*

(JAMES 2:1)

*"Hearken, my beloved brethren, Hath not God chosen the poor of this world **rich in faith**, and heirs of the kingdom which he hath promised to them that love him?"*

(JAMES 2:5)

*"What doth it profit, my brethren, though a man say he hath **faith**, and have not works? can **faith** save him?"*

(JAMES 2:14)

*"Even so **faith**, if it hath not works, is dead, being alone."*

(JAMES 2:17)

*"Yea, a man may say, Thou hast **faith**, and I have works: shew me thy **faith** without thy works, and I will shew thee my **faith** by my works."*

(JAMES 2:18)

*"But wilt thou know, O vain man, that **faith** without works is dead?"*

(JAMES 2:20)

*"Seest thou how **faith** wrought with his works, and by works was **faith** made perfect?"*

(JAMES 2:22)

*"For as the body without the spirit is dead, so **faith** without works is dead also."*

(JAMES 2:26)

*"And the prayer of **faith** shall save the sick, and the Lord shall raise him up; and if he have committed sins, they shall be forgiven him."*

(JAMES 5:15)

*"Who are kept by the power of God through **faith** unto salvation ready to be revealed in the last time."*

(1 PETER 1:5)

*"That the trial of your **faith**, being much more precious than of gold that perisheth, though it be tried with fire, might be found unto praise and honor and glory at the appearing of Jesus Christ."*

(1 PETER 1:7)

*"Who by him do believe in God, that raised him up from the dead, and gave him glory; that **your faith** and hope might be in God."*

(1 PETER 1:21)

*"Simon Peter, a servant and an apostle of Jesus Christ, to them that have obtained like **precious faith** with us through the righteousness of God and our Saviour Jesus Christ."*

(2 PETER 1:1)

*"And beside this, giving all diligence, add to your **faith** virtue; and to virtue knowledge."*

(2 PETER 1:5)

*"I know thy works, and where thou dwellest, even where Satan's seat is: and thou holdest fast my name, and hast not denied my **faith**, even in those days wherein Antipas was my faithful martyr, who was slain among you, where Satan dwelleth."*

(REVELATION 2:13)

*"I know thy works, and charity, and service, and **faith**, and thy patience, and thy works; and the last to be more than the first."*

(REVELATION 2:19)

*"He that leadeth into captivity shall go into captivity: he that killeth with the sword must be killed with the sword. Here is the patience and the **faith** of the saints."*

(REVELATION 13:10)

*"Here is the patience of the saints: here are they that keep the commandments of God, and the **faith of Jesus**."*

(REVELATION 14:12)

We hope you enjoyed reading this New Wine book.
For details of other New Wine books
and a range of 2,000 titles from other
Spirit-filled publishers visit our website:
www.newwineministries.co.uk